High Heels

OrangeBooks Publication

1st Floor, Rajhans Arcade, Mall Road, Kohka, Bhilai, Chhattisgarh 490020
Website: **www.orangebooks.in**

First Edition, 2025

ISBN: 978-93-6554-927-0

Price: Rs. 399.00

Printed in India

A MEMOIR

HIGH HEELS

Where Resilience Wears Hope.

Muna Dadel

OrangeBooks Publication

www.orangebooks.in

Dedication

To Adhyan and Saisha - you are the reason I kept walking, even barefoot through storms.

May you always walk tall — in truth, in love, and in your dreams.

To V. Sairam — who gave me back my wings.

To everyone who helped me, and those who didn't — you shaped me.

To my parents and in-laws — for your roots and prayers.

To Pima, Yashoda, Vishnu, and Sujan — for the laughter of childhood.

To Jagruti — who reminded me of who I am.

And to my Maa — I hope heaven has books, so you can read this too.

Preface

High Heels

"She didn't wear heels to impress — she wore them to rise."

This is not just my story.

It's ours.

It belongs to the ones who've loved quietly, fallen without applause, and risen without a stage.

To those who've broken in silence and healed in pieces.

To those who've walked through life in borrowed shoes, with empty pockets or swollen hearts — but still kept walking.

We may not have medals. We may not be known.

But our stories matter.

This book isn't about being perfect or successful.

It's about being real.

About feeling too much.

About carrying invisible weights with invisible courage.

About choosing to hope, even on the days it would've been easier to give up.

If you've ever felt unseen, unheard, or uncertain — this is for you.

Let's walk together, page by page.

— ***Muna Dadel***

Contents

Chapter - 1

Dream vs. Diagrams

"The biggest adventure you can take is to live the life of your dreams."

— Oprah Winfrey

I stepped out of a sleek black car, its glossy surface catching the midday sun. My red high heels, fierce and unapologetic, sparked like stars—the kind I once admired from afar, never dreaming that they'd one day carry me.

Tak... tak... tak.

Each click of my heels echoed on the gleaming marble, a drumroll for my arrival.

The office lobby greeted me like royalty. Off-white walls whispered elegance. Gold accents shimmered. Couches curved like clouds. A massive chandelier spilt rose-gold light, like magic falling from the ceiling. A cluster of green plants stood beside a vase so perfect it looked like it had its own stylist. Orchids leaned out, bowing—as if to welcome me. A soft floral scent wrapped around me, not too sweet, not too strong. Just right.

Heads turned. Maybe someone whispered, "She's here." But I didn't need the words. I felt it. In that moment, beneath the hush of heels and perfume, I stepped into my future—bold, beautiful, entirely mine.

TRINGGGG! TRINGGGG!

The school bell shrieked. The fan slowed to a lazy crawl. The light flickered. Heat barged in like an uninvited guest. The dream was shattered. The free period was over—and with it, my fantasy.

Back to real life. Back to Class 8B in a small school in Dombivli, a modest city on the outskirts of Mumbai.

I was there, on a scratched brown wooden bench in the middle row. My hair pulled so tight that even my thoughts felt stretched. A school bag heavier than my will to study. The geography textbook lay open in front of me. My mind? Still lingering in that golden lobby, shining red high heels, surrounded by orchids and silence.

I was Muna—a girl with a colourful pen, a restless imagination, and stories no syllabus ever wanted. My tight black shoes squashed my toes. Sweat pooled under my collar. And then—she walked in—our teacher. Carrying the thickest textbook mankind has ever produced.

The Battlefield of Subjects

My grades were a battlefield. Geography was the most joyless subject in the known universe, with no hero, no plot twist, just borders, rivers, and boredom. Ma'am scanned the room like a villain hunting prey, her eyes narrowing over her half-down glasses. "Where is Australia?" She barked. I panicked, pointing vaguely in the direction of Austria. The class laughed. Honestly, who named those countries so similarly? It's all one big, pointless puzzle. If the world wanted kids to remember geography, it should've let eighth graders name the countries. We'd have "Castle land" and "Jump town."

Math was a cold case with no closure. Every chapter began with the same mystery: Find X. Who lost it? Why is it my job to bring it back? I don't even know X! Geometry? Please. Some ancient mathematician—holding a grudge against children—wrote a theorem in a language even Google Translate fears. Trigonometry? Sin, cos, theta? Sorry, I don't speak alien code. I barely understood Math, but at least I knew this much: the square root of my patience was a perfect zero.

Science was fun, sometimes. Especially the practicals, like the day they casually announced, "The heart of a shrimp is in its head." Excuse me?! So, shrimps think with their hearts? Thanks to science, I had a water pet named H_2O and a salt crystal with a nickname longer than my family tree. Why call it 'sodium chloride' when 'salt' works just fine? The universe was full of secrets, but the only one I ever truly cared about was how to make this class end faster.

History felt like a 300-part series where everyone dies, and you're expected to remember every single date. Exams made it worse. "Write a short note on the Harappan Civilisation." Me: "They were civilised. Isn't that enough?" Archaeology felt like grave-robbing with permission. Digging up the bones of people who didn't want to be found. I'm pretty sure their ghosts are still in the archives, rearranging the dates just to mess with us.

When Marks Fail, But Family Doesn't

My struggle with these subjects eventually caught up with me. It was the seventh standard. First unit test. I barely passed in math and failed Social Studies. That chapter on medieval India—Delhi Sultanate, new kingdoms, Mughal Empire—was a royal mess of names and dates. My paper came back so red, it could've triggered a fire alarm.

The teacher announced, "Whoever failed must call their parents."

Call Maa? Even when I passed, she scolded me for not topping.

So, like any desperate 12-year-old, I plotted a heist. My friend—who had failed four subjects (a true legend)—offered her neighbour to act as my aunt. "Wow, that sounds like a plan, and I will forge a signature," I said.

Mission Fake PTM: Activated.

But fate had better drama in store. The day before the PTM, I forgot my tiffin.

Guess who showed up at school? Maa. Holding my lunchbox like a ticking bomb.

She smiled sweetly, handed it to me… Then walked straight to my class teacher.

I stood frozen at my bench, every second stretching like a chewing gum in summer. I couldn't hear their conversation, but I didn't need to. I imagined every possible horror: Expulsion. Shame. Crying. Maybe a lifetime ban from cartoons.

My hands were cold. My stomach? Doing somersaults.

By the time school ended, I was drenched—not from heat, but from imagining my funeral. I walked home like I was heading toward judgment day.

Every door creaked, every glance from Maa felt like a clue that she knew. That evening, I came home with heavy steps and a heavier heart. Baba was sitting on the sofa, waiting for me. From his expression, I could tell—Maa had already given him the full report. Not just the marks, but the drama that followed.

He didn't shout. He didn't raise his voice or his eyebrows. That made it even scarier.

Maa, on the other hand, her calm broke like a thunderclap. One look and I knew—Kali Ma mode was on.

But just before the storm hit, Baba quietly lifted his hand. He wasn't loud. He wasn't angry. He was just still. And somehow, that stillness made even Maa stop.

"I'm not worried about the marks," he said. "But I want to understand—what happened? Why did you lie, Muna?"

That was the first time I saw disappointment without anger. And it stung.

I didn't have an answer. His voice broke me. I looked down.

"Because… I didn't want to disappoint you."

He wiped my cheek. Smiled gently. "You're a good student, Muna. You just need to focus." Then, softer—"It's just a unit test. If it were finals, you'd repeat. But this? This is just a chapter. Not your story."

Maa, still fiery, pulled me into a tight hug. "I'm not angry you failed. I'm hurt you hid it. Marks we can fix. Broken trust? That's harder to erase than red ink."

I survived. And thank God I didn't pull the fake-aunty stunt. Knowing Maa, she would've hung me like drying laundry… Then scolded the neighbour, too.

Lesson learned: Don't lie. Don't fail it—whatever it is. And never—never—forget your tiffin.

I wasn't the class topper. And I wasn't the quiet one either.

I laughed too loudly. Helped too many. Talked too much. And dreamed far too wild for a classroom.

It wasn't just about what was written in those textbooks. It was about what was missing.

I wasn't made for maps. I was made for moments.

The girl with the colored dreams wasn't raised to just follow rules. She was raised by a man with a broken cape and an unbroken will, and a woman whose fierce love was a fortress.

Lessons Beyond the Bell

Bright dreams dimmed as the school bell cried,
Its echo is lost in the noise outside.
They gave me facts, a measured pace,
But my heart was running its own race.

My dreams were stitched from paper and ink,
Not the lines they told me to think.
Each scribbled word, each fearless try,
Built wings that reached a higher sky.

My parents' hands, both strong and kind,
Taught me to trust my seeking mind:
Each hard lesson, big or small,
Is not the end—it's just the wall you scale to rise above it all.

Chapter - 2

My Superhero with a Torn Cape

"Some heroes wear capes. Mine wore dusty shoes, carried tired eyes, and built dreams with bare hands."

— Muna Dadel

We didn't grow up with branded shoes or birthday balloons. But we never felt poor.

Because in our home, love was loud and constant. It spilt into lunchboxes, auto rides, and evening laughter—even when money stayed quiet.

There were seven of us—a big brother, two younger sisters, one little hurricane of a brother, and me. The second child, forever wedged between the expectations of the eldest and the chaos of the middle.

Daju, our eldest, lived like he was born with a crown. He never adjusted, never settled, always reaching for more—as if some royal destiny was waiting just outside the city limits.

Pima, my younger sister, was a spark plug: short-tempered, sharp-tongued, and pure-hearted. She'd pick a fight in the blink of an eye, but the moment Maa fed her with her hands, she melted like butter on warm roti.

Then there was **Yashoda**—Yashu, the little fairy of our family. Delicate, fair-skinned, and graceful in her silence. She didn't speak much, and when she did, it was with intention. Baba called her the "light of our house."

And **Vishnu**—the youngest storm. Naughty beyond measure. He didn't speak for the first few years, no matter what Maa tried—herbal remedies, whispered mantras, borrowed prayers. And then, just like that, one day he spoke—and never stopped. I still remember the day he lost a tooth while playing. After a painful dental visit, his revenge plan was clear and dramatic:

"One day I'll become a dentist and take out this doctor's teeth!"

Each of us was wildly different. But together, we were Baba's biggest reason to keep going.

Baba – The Real Superhero

My Baba wasn't a man who showed off. He was a man who showed up.

He worked as a security guard—nothing glamorous, nothing high-paying. But every time he wore that uniform, it felt like watching a soldier suit up. It wasn't just a job; it was a promise he made to us every single day. He came home each night with tired feet but unshaken hope. No matter how hard the day, he never left his smile at the gate.

Some evenings, I'd sit quietly at the window, my cheek pressed against the metal grill, watching the flickering streetlight and waiting for his footsteps. When they finally echoed up the stairwell, I'd run back to bed and pretend to be asleep.

He always knew.

A gentle pat on the head, and his tired voice would whisper, "Sutis nani?"—Are you asleep*?* I wouldn't answer. But inside, I smiled. Because nothing felt more like home than hearing my name in his tired whisper.

A Promise, A Home

When I was born, we lived in a slum—a place where children learned curse words before the alphabet, and lullabies got drowned out by shouting.

But something shifted in Baba the day he held me. He looked at his newborn daughter—his princess—and made a quiet promise: "She won't grow up here."

And he kept it.

Before I turned nine months old, he bought a one-room flat in a decent building. At that time, only Daju and I were born. It wasn't big. It wasn't luxurious. But it was clean. Safer. Ours. Maa often retold the story of that move—not just because it was a new address, but because it brought her dignity. For the first time, she didn't have to wake at 4 a.m. to carry heavy buckets from a distant tap. There was running water in our own kitchen.

To her, that gentle flow wasn't just convenience—it was freedom.

She'd cradle baby me in one arm, fill a glass in the other, and smile like she owned the world. That memory became one of her favourite bedtime stories, passed down like a family heirloom, not for the place, but for the pride it gave her.

Thief in the Palace

Life zigzagged—joy and chaos often danced too close together. But as long as we were together, we felt rich.

Our new building was still under construction—a G+3 with only two families moved in. We lived on the ground floor, and our balcony? Half-open. Easy to jump over. Which someone did.

The very first night in our new home, Baba left for night duty. In the silence of midnight, our house got a strange welcome: a thief.

He slipped in through the open balcony while we slept. There wasn't much to steal—maybe five hundred rupees and a few silver ornaments. But Maa sensed something. She stayed still, holding her breath like a warrior in wait.

When the thief stepped into the room, purse in hand, my usually soft-spoken mother rose like fire.

In one bold move, she slammed the sliding door shut and locked it with shaking hands.

Then she screamed—not in fear, but fury.

The thief fled.

If he was new at this, he picked the wrong house—and the wrong mother.

The next morning, Baba came home and installed iron grills. Safety first. Always.

Maa would retell the story over the years, her voice rising in a dramatic climax as she described locking the thief in. It became our family's favourite legend. Pima would gasp and exclaim, "Maa, you're so brave!" Daju, ever the protective eldest, would puff out his chest and declare that he would have chased the thief away himself. Yashu, with her gentle and unique perspective, would say, "Poor thief, he must have been thinking he didn't get anything after all that hard work." And Vishnu, always the loudest, would simply declare, "Wow, my Maa is the best."

To us, that story wasn't about a thief or a loss of money. It was about our mother's courage, a reminder that our home was a fortress, not just of iron bars, but of fierce, protective love.

The Diwali That Almost Wasn't

Baba wasn't unbreakable. I saw it once—just once.

It was just before Diwali. Usually, we'd begin planning months in advance—comparing prices, chasing sales, searching for the perfect shades. But that year, things were tight. The rickshaw needed repairs. School fees had piled up. Grandma was unwell.

One evening, I saw Baba sitting on the balcony floor, staring into the breeze, a newspaper rustling in his hand. He hadn't changed out of his uniform. His face was quiet—too quiet.

I sat beside him and whispered, "I don't need a new dress this year, Baba. I'll get one next time."

He turned to me slowly. His eyes were wet, but he didn't blink the tears away.

"I'm proud of you," he said.

Back then, I just thought he was being kind. But now I know—it was one of those moments that broke a father's heart a little. Because he couldn't give. And because I understood.

That night, we didn't talk much. But the silence said everything.

Ten days later, a dress appeared on my pillow—folded with care, its tag hanging by a thread, as if someone had left a secret there for me to discover. When I tried it on, it didn't just fit my body; it fit my silence, my waiting.

Sunday Santa

While most fathers rested on Sundays, mine changed uniforms.

After long shifts as a security guard, Baba would drive an auto-rickshaw. His back was sore. His eyes were red. But his spirit? Unshaken.

He didn't work extra for luxuries. He worked to cover our school fees, EMI, medicines, and Maa's quiet dreams.

And once a month, like magic, he became our Sunday Santa.

He'd take us on joyrides in his auto—his kingdom on three wheels, and we, the royal parade. Parks, dusty fields, kite chases. He'd race with us like a child and laugh with us like we had nothing to worry about.

At sunset, we'd stop for chaat—spicy, tangy, tongue-burning. It made us cough and giggle, crying from the heat, begging for more. Just like life: sometimes harsh, sometimes sour, always memorable—especially when shared.

The Cake That Taught Me My Worth

Some lessons come wrapped in celebration. Others come wrapped in hurt.

Mine came wrapped in vanilla frosting.

I was seven—carefree, playful, unaware of how the world could wound without warning. One evening, as I walked home after playing, I noticed a party at our neighbour's house. Music thumped. Laughter echoed. Lights glittered. Curious, I peeked in through the door.

Someone saw me and smiled. They called me in, handed me a slice of cake—soft, creamy, rich with sugar and excitement. I held it like a treasure and ran home.

But Baba saw.

Without a word, he slapped me lightly on the back. The cake fell. I burst into tears—loud, confused, heartbroken. Maa held me, trying to calm me down.

Later, Baba came and sat beside me. He applied balm to my back and wiped my tears.

"They called me in," I whispered between sniffles.

"No," he said gently. "They called you only because you were peeking. That cake wasn't meant for you. You were not their first choice."

There was no anger in his voice—just quiet pain.

"I never want you to feel like someone's second option," he continued. "Not for cake. Not for love. Not for life."

That day, I didn't just learn not to peek into someone's house. I learned never to peek into someone's life, hoping to be invited. I learned self-worth. And what it means when someone protects your dignity, even if through discipline.

The Peda

But the moment etched deepest in my heart? It wasn't a festival or a fancy day. It was a single **peda**.

Whenever someone at Baba's office celebrated—a birthday, promotion, a new scooter—they brought sweets. Most people ate and moved on. But Baba? He'd wrap that one peda in paper—newspaper, sometimes plastic—and carry it home like a treasure.

He never ate it alone. Not even a bite.

He'd sit cross-legged on the floor, still in his dusty uniform, and call us: Maa, Daju, me, Pima, Yashu, and little Vishnu. We'd all gather like a circle around a miracle.

He'd unwrap the peda slowly, as if it were sacred, and break it into tiny, uneven pieces—yet somehow, it was always enough. No one got the bigger share. Not even him.

Because what he truly savoured wasn't the sweet. It was the moment. He never had everything. But he gave us more than enough. Because love does math differently.

The Dream Diary

You know where I learned to dream? From him.

In the early 90s—no mobile phones, no Pinterest boards, no Instagram reels—Baba had something better. A simple company diary.

Each Diwali, he received one. Plain, with blue lines and a plastic cover that curled in the summer heat.

Most used it for groceries or attendance logs. But Baba turned it into a vault of dreams.

Inside: our names, birthdays, and tiny notes only a father would think to write. Then came the clippings—torn from old magazines and newspapers: villas with wide verandas, tulsi-lined paths, golden light spilling from windows.

Homes we'd never seen—but Baba visited them often. In his mind. In his plans.

He didn't just wish. He mapped. Room by room. Brick by brick.

That diary didn't hold records. It held belief.

Most people write what is. Baba wrote what could be.

Even now, when I dream of something wild—a new city, a book, a better life—I see his handwriting in the back of my mind. Neat. Hopeful. Unshaken.

A man with a pocket full of coins, a head full of worries, and no backup plan—still made space for dreams. To him, dreaming wasn't a luxury. It was a responsibility. He taught me that magic doesn't live in fairy tales. It lives in peda crumbs, sweaty auto rides, and pencilled floor plans. He made the impossible look gentle. Years later, I tried to explain who he was—how he carried dreams like grocery bags. But words failed me. So, I wrote this poem instead, because sometimes the deepest truths are not explained, but felt—in the rhythm and heart of a story.

Worn but Unbroken – My Superhero

Not forged in war, nor made for fame,

He rose through life's unending game.

No medals shone upon his chest —

Just steady hands and quiet rest.

His cape was years old, worn soft and thin,

His sword — the will he kept within.

He spoke in actions, seldom in sound,

Yet his silence made my world go round.

No dragons slain, no jewelled crown,

Yet he lifted me each time I fell down.

A lighthouse through my fiercest tide,

He stood with love, unshaken beside.

Through storms, he walked with empty hands,

Still built my dreams on shifting sands.

He gave far more than roof or bread —

He gave me the strength to rise instead

Chapter - 3

The Barefoot Queen with Eight Hands

"A parent's love calculates in silence — subtracting from their needs to multiply yours."

— Muna

Long before I knew what queens or warriors looked like, I met my mother. She didn't wear crowns or carry swords — just a steel spatula seasoned with stories, eight invisible hands, and a voice that could turn chaos into calm.

Sometimes, when I watch serene Japanese school videos—children marching in neat lines, sweeping classrooms like tiny monks, carrying tiffins with the solemnity of diplomats — I smile and think:

"They must've met my mother in another life. Or worse—she trained them."

Because my mother? She didn't just believe in discipline—she was discipline.

A one-woman army with a belan seasoned by rotis and rebellion, and a saree that flowed like a battle flag. She didn't run a household. She ran an empire.

No alarms. No reminders. Just her — always on time, never offbeat. A walking timetable with eyes that scanned tiffin boxes, lost socks, and bad lies in a single glance.

The Clockwork of Her Silence

She rose at 5 AM — no alarm, no fuss, no "five more minutes." Not even on Sundays. Her breath moved in sync with the rhythm of the day: boiling milk, folding clothes, lighting the lamp, prepping tiffins — all before the sun yawned.

She pressed our uniforms with steam that matched her breath, braided hair while stirring milk, and hummed bhajans between scoldings and instructions. No cape. Just a dupatta tucked tight at the waist like a battle sash.

No house help. No school bus. No shortcuts.

Just her — soft-soled on the cool floor, belan in one hand, the entire universe in the other.

Our kitchen wasn't modular — it was magical. A place where leftovers became feasts, gossip sizzled with the tadka, and love had its aroma, stronger than any spice.

She didn't sleep before 11. Nineteen hours of spinning like a top — only, even tops get to fall. She didn't.

We weren't rich in things. But oh, we were royalty in spirit.

Our home was a scene from an old Hindi movie. Faded curtains danced gently in the ceiling fan's breeze — tired, but graceful, like an old saree still catching the light.

The soft clink of steel plates echoed through the room — a humble orchestra of lunchtime rituals. No luxury, but everything shone — scrubbed clean with love, lined up like proud soldiers on a kitchen shelf.

And in the quiet between each clang, our empty stomachs joined the rhythm, grumbling like backup singers, waiting for the chorus of rice and daal.

The Kheer War: Sweet Chaos and Flying Spoons

One golden Sunday, Mom decided to make kheer — the kind that wraps the whole house in a warm, saffron-cardamom hug. Milk bubbled like a lullaby, rice danced gently within, and sugar melted into memory. The aroma alone could've turned enemies into best friends.

We — four hungry wolves (Vishnu wasn't born yet) in school shorts — sniffed our way to the kitchen like detectives chasing dessert.

She poured the kheer into five steel bowls. One for each of us. And the last — always the smallest — for herself. That was her rule: *"Mothers eat last. Sometimes never."*

I held my bowl like a sacred offering and tiptoed to sip water from the matka. Without thinking, I placed the bowl beside it.

And then... the storm broke.

My elder brother — His Royal Highness, Prince of Pouting — peered into his bowl and gasped.

"Mummy! Hers is fuller than mine!"

Maa turned slowly. Not angry — amused. Dangerous.

"Next time I'll buy a gold scale to measure rice," she said, calm as a storm that knows it's coming.

But oh no. He had summoned the beast.

Spoon-counting began. Spoon-counting. Like a kheer auditor. Like the Income Tax Department of desserts.

Maa took one breath — then BAM!

"Here! Take this, and this — in fact, take it ALL! Want more? Climb up and pull it off the ceiling too! If we were rich, I'd be flinging glass bowls at you — but thank your stars, poverty saved your head today!"

Steel bowls flew like missiles. Kheer splashed across walls. One bowl did a full flip. A spoon clanged against the fridge.

Her voice cracked with that strange mix — I could see the anger, yet hidden inside it was her helpless way of trying to make us laugh, to lighten the moment. But anger always won in the end. She'd feel bad afterward, while we sat frozen, caught between fear and guilt.

Meanwhile, my forgotten bowl near the matka sat untouched, quietly glowing in its corner of survival. The lone survivor in a battlefield of rice and regret.

And that's when the giggles began.

A small one. Then another.

Soon, we were in full-blown, belly-aching, tear-streaming laughter.

In the end, we all gathered around that single saved bowl—sharing it like prasad, licking our fingers like it was the last supper.

That day wasn't about dessert. It was about everything she held inside—the pressure, the love, the impossible balance.

She wasn't throwing kheer. She was throwing out the myth that mothers must always be calm, composed, and quiet.

And in that sweet storm, we didn't just see our Maa —

We saw the woman behind her. Loud. Exhausted. Glorious.

The Vegetable That Scared Me to Bravery

I must've been five, maybe six — that age when monsters hid under beds, not in vegetables.

One afternoon, Maa served bitter gourd for lunch. Karela. Even the name sounded cruel, like a punishment wrapped in green. It looked like a wrinkled monster and tasted like betrayal in every bite.

I sat at the edge of my plate, arms crossed, lips curled, face twisted like a crushed drawing I didn't want anyone to see. Maa looked at me — calm, amused — and said gently:

"Food should be eaten with a smile… otherwise, it gets angry. If you frown while eating, the food will never come to you again. It doesn't like sad faces — it finds joy and goes where it's welcomed."

I froze. Food… gets angry?

My little brain panicked. Would the karela yell at me? Complain to Maa? Come alive at night?

Frightened but obedient, I picked it up with trembling fingers — like defusing a bomb — and forced the biggest, toothiest smile I could manage.

And then I ate it. Chewing slowly. Eyes wide. Smiling like a hostage in a vegetable negotiation.

Maa didn't scold. She didn't push. She just sat across, biting her lip, holding back a laugh that nearly spilt from her eyes.

Back then, I believed she was smiling with me.

Now I know — she was smiling at me.

At my innocence. At my terror. At my tiny, trembling victory over bitterness.

And maybe… that's what she always wanted for us.

Not just to taste life's sweetness —

But to learn how to swallow the bitter, too.

With courage. With grace. With a crooked little smile.

The Day Her Hand Spoke Louder Than Words

I was the laziest of us all — the "five more minutes, Ma" child, the unofficial snooze-button ambassador.

For years, she tried every gentle method:

First call: a soft voice.

Second: a gentle shake.

Third: "Wake up, Muna…"

Fourth: "Beta, please…"

I knew she had tried everything else. I knew patience had run its course.

And then came that day.

She called once. Twice.

Then... SLAP.

Right on the cheek. Sharp, unexpected, yet calm — a sting that woke not just my body, but my mind. I didn't cry. I just stared, stunned by the truth in her eyes more than the pain on my skin.

She whispered, her voice steady:

"Life doesn't wait for sleepy heads. That day, I learned: if you want to rise, you must wake yourself — inside and out."

Since that day, I have never needed five calls. One whisper from her is enough. Even now, before dawn, I sometimes hear her voice in the wind —

"Muna… uthi ja nani…"

And I rise — not out of habit, but out of honour.

The Name That Made Me Smile

I never liked my name. Everyone had beautiful, long, magical names — and mine? Short, weird, and easy to tease. Boys in school would yell, "Oyee Munna!" and laugh until their faces hurt. Even teachers would double-check my name on attendance sheets, and I'd shrink into my chair, ashamed.

One day, I marched straight to Maa and asked, "Why Muna? Why me?"

She looked at me calmly, as if the answer was obvious. "Your moon sign is Leo, so your name had to start with M," she said.

I huffed. "A thousand names start with M! Why Muna? Because of you, everyone laughs at me!"

She smiled, that quiet, secretive smile that made you pause before she spoke. "In Nepali, Muna means a person whom everyone loves — a lovable person. No other name will suit you. Let them laugh; don't bother. You're meant to be loved, no matter what they say."

Something in her words — her certainty, her warmth — made my chest swell. I felt like I had won a small, private victory. I smiled, proud, confident… and carried that pride for years.

Years later, when I looked it up on Google, I found that "Muna" means new and tender. Maa's sweet little lie had done its magic — and that was enough.

Her Crown Was Patience, Her Sword –a Belan

Even today, as I juggle messy mornings — half-packed tiffins, forgotten keys, mismatched socks — I wonder how she did it all. Barefoot. Smiling. With no vacation, no me time, no applause.

Then I remember: she didn't need a crown.

She ruled with eight invisible hands, a belan seasoned by parathas and discipline, and a will forged in fire.

She wasn't trying to raise perfect kids. She was building character — quietly, stubbornly, lovingly.

Through every spilt kheer, every frown at a bitter karela, every gentle slap, and every clever way she made me love my name, I learned who my mother truly was. She wasn't just running a household — she was building character, shaping resilience, and teaching us how to face life with courage and grace. Fearless in her decisions, unwavering in her discipline, and overflowing with love, she ruled not with medals or crowns, but with patience, wisdom, and a heart that never tired. This was my mother — the barefoot queen with eight invisible hands, the woman who made our world run smoothly while showing us how to rise, laugh, and stand tall.

The Unstoppable Force.

No throne, no medals, no songs sung in her name,

Yet storms bowed down to her quiet flame.

She built warriors, not dolls or charms,

With love as her armour and discipline as arms.

Her footsteps carved paths where courage could grow,

Her eyes held the truth we needed to know.

Through spilt kheer, bitter karela, and tireless days,

She forged our hearts in unyielding ways.

Barefoot and fearless, she ruled every fight,

Turning ordinary moments into radiant light.

No glory, no fanfare, no banners unfurled,

Yet she was, and always will be, the queen of our world.

Chapter - 4

The Empty Sky

*"Not all storms come with thunder —
some arrive in silence."*

Some days don't arrive like gentle mornings.

They crash into your life like uninvited storms — no forecast, no mercy.

It's not easy to write about the days I wish I could erase—days that felt like ink stains on a white page. But maybe... some stories don't want to be buried. Maybe they aren't meant to be forgotten. Maybe they need to be freed — like a prayer caught in the throat for far too long.

It was Janmashtami. Lord Krishna's birthday. A day we waited for with childlike joy and quiet reverence. In our home, it was more than a festival — it was tradition stitched with emotion.

We would fast as a family — me, my sister, Baba, and Maa Maa— dressed in simplicity, our hearts draped in faith. At midnight, we'd gather for the aarti, the soft flame of the diya dancing in rhythm with the bhajans. The air would smell of incense and camphor. Maa would lead the prayers with unmatched enthusiasm — singing aloud, swaying gently, her eyes sparkling like she could see Krishna himself smiling back at her.

After the aarti, we'd offer prasad — a bowl of mixed fruits, kheer, sweets, and her soft puris that somehow always tasted better that night. The night would end with the comforting clatter of plates and the warm joy of food—a well-earned reward after fasting.

We would laugh about who cheated — a secret bite of fruit, an extra sip of water. But somehow, with Maa's Maa presence and Krishna's name on our lips, even hunger felt sacred.

But that year… none of it happened.

No midnight bhajans.

No aarti.

No kheer simmering in the kitchen.

Without Maa's excitement, the night felt hollow. The house was silent, not peaceful, but empty. Like a painting stripped of colour. Like a melody that forgot its tune. We didn't say it aloud, but we all felt it: Janmashtami hadn't arrived. Not really. Because the soul of our celebration—the one who made faith feel festive—was fading right in front of us.

That morning, she had still woken up at 5 a.m., as always. But her movements were slow, like her body was borrowing time it didn't have. Her hands trembled slightly while making tea. Her eyes, usually bright with mischief and purpose, looked dull, like the diya had gone out.

Baba noticed. He stood quietly near the doorway, watching her with growing worry.

“Don’t fast today,” he said gently, as though afraid to disturb something fragile.

“Please rest. I’ll come home early. We’ll go see the doctor.”

He wanted to stay. His silence said so. But duty rarely waits for heartache. With five children and a mountain of responsibilities,he gently patted Maa’s head — a wordless way of saying he cared. and stepped out, trusting in hope and habit.

That evening, they visited the doctor.

“Just fatigue,” they said.

A few tests. Nothing urgent.

But the next morning, the air shifted.

Her face was swollen. Her lips were pale. And then she began to vomit — again and again.

This time, I saw it.

There was blood. Not just red, but wrong. It didn’t belong there. Not beside the Tulsi plant or the half-folded laundry.

Not in our story. Not like this.

Baba didn’t ask questions. He just threw on the first shirt he could find, grabbed his wallet, and rushed out to get an auto, like the house was on fire. Inside, Maa was getting ready.

Not with panic, but with quiet purpose.

Like she was packing for something longer than a hospital stay. She reached for her favourite blue saree, the one with the thin silver border. Her hands trembled as she tried to comb her hair, then turned to me.

“Help me comb it,” she whispered.

She had never asked that before.

It was always her fingers in our hair, her oil-slicked hands parting the strands with care. But that day, for the first time, the comb passed from her hand to mine. I sat behind her and gently combed her hair, each stroke brushing away a piece of my childhood.

She adjusted her saree, placed a maroon bindi on her forehead, and sat down on the bed. Her breathing was heavier now, but she still smiled — faintly — like she was trying to protect us from the truth her body had already accepted.

Then she pulled us close. All five of us.

Yashoda was just ten. Vishnu, seven. The moment they looked into her eyes — red, distant, swollen with unspoken words—they broke. Their tears came fast, unfiltered.

She kissed them long and deep, as if she were pouring all the mothering she had left into that one moment. Pima, our sharp-tongued, fiery thirteen-year-old, tried to lighten the air.

"Arrey, why are you both crying?" she said. "Maa will be back in two days — healthy and shouting again."

But I couldn't say a word.

Maa looked at me, not with fear, but something heavier: acceptance.

She cupped my cheek and said softly:

"Muna… I don't think I'll come back."

I froze. Her words — soft, sharp, final — pierced through the room like a silent scream. Something inside me recoiled. I wanted to scream at her — to tell her not to say such things, not today, not on Janmashtami.

But I couldn't. Because somewhere, a crack had already formed in my belief. And that scared me more than her words.

"You'll have to take care of your brothers and sisters," she said. "Baba will go to work… someone has to hold the house."

I didn't believe her. I couldn't.

She had said things like this before, whenever she was upset:

"You'll only understand when I'm gone."

I thought this was just another one of those moments.

Then —

Beep… Beep… Beep.

The auto horn. Baba had returned.

Maa wiped her tears with the corner of her saree — slow, deliberate — as if clearing the last trace of her fear. She adjusted her bindi with trembling fingers, like she was putting herself together one last time.

Then she stood up.

And smiled.

Not the kind of smile that comes from joy, but the kind mothers wear when they're protecting everyone but themselves.

A smile stitched together with surrender.

Like a curtain falling after the final act — graceful, quiet, irreversible.

And then… she hugged us.

One by one. And then all at once.

Tight. Too tight.

As if she was pressing pieces of herself into our skin — her warmth, her memory, her smell, her strength.

It wasn't just a hug.

It was a transfer.

Of love. Of legacy. Of goodbye.

That evening felt unfamiliar. Like the house had forgotten how to breathe.

There was no pressure cooker whistle.

No bangles clinking against steel thalis.

No gentle scolding about school bags.

No "Drink your milk before it gets cold."

Just stillness.

And the ticking of a clock that suddenly felt too loud. Too cruel.

Her presence had always been quietly stitched into our routines — without her, even the walls looked confused.

The kitchen waited. The stove stayed untouched.

Even the small temple — the one she cleaned each morning — looked… incomplete.

We moved like shadows. Like we were underwater — slow, silent, unsure if this was real or some half-dream we couldn't wake from.

I asked softly,

"Baba, what did the doctor say?"

He looked at me, paused, then looked away.

"Nothing much," he replied, with a smile that didn't reach his eyes.

"She'll be alright soon."

But something about the way he said it felt strange — like he was hiding something he wasn't ready to say.

Later, I found out what the doctor had said:

"It's difficult to save her," he told Baba.

"But we can try. Her body is young, just 32. We need to put her on a ventilator."

And still, Baba had protected us with silence.

My siblings were unusually quiet. Books lay open, but no pages were turned.

Nobody fought over the remote.

Nobody asked what was for dinner.

And me?

I kept thinking about her saree — the baby pink one with purple lily flowers and a soft satin border.

She had bought it just a few weeks ago, said she'd wear it on a "good day."

It still hung behind the door, untouched — like a dream she didn't get to live in.

And then — the strangest thing.

I kept hearing her voice.

Not loud. Not clear.

But there.

Like a whisper curling around the corners of the room.

Like she was saying something only my heart could catch.

I turned around.

No one.

Nothing.

Just silence pretending to be her.

And that hug — that last, too-tight hug — kept playing on repeat inside my chest.

The next morning, I went to the temple to pray for her.

As I stepped out, I noticed a lone mynah bird perched quietly on the temple gate. A friend once told me that spotting a pair of mynahs together was a sign of good luck. Before exams, we'd look for them — and oddly enough, we always ended up doing well. But seeing just one? That was said to bring bad luck.

I know it's just superstition. But that morning, I couldn't stop myself from believing it. I searched the trees, electric wires, and rooftops — hoping the second bird would show up. It never did.

A strange fear settled in. That evening, there was a tightness in my chest. Not quite pain — just a heavy, unexplained weight. Like something had shifted. Like a quiet storm had started inside me.

It wasn't fear.

It wasn't a worry.

It was something deeper.

Heavier.

Unamenable.

It felt like the silence inside me had started to scream.

I turned to my cousin and said:

"Let's go to the hospital. I don't know why… but I need to see her."

Hospitals are built to preserve life, but no one talks about how lifeless they feel. The fluorescent lights stung my eyes. A child cried in a nearby ward. Somewhere, metal scraped against metal — a tray or a wheelchair, I couldn't tell. My slippers stuck slightly to the disinfected floor. The whole place smelled like decisions no one wanted to make.

I saw Baba.
My superhero.
The man who never bent, never broke.

Not standing tall.
Not holding the weight of the world like always.

But sitting.
On a bench.
In the corner.

Head down.
Eyes flooded.
Fists clenched.

He looked up — and I saw it.
The crack. The heartbreak.
The helplessness of a man who had always been the pillar of our home, now collapsing silently in a public hallway.

I rushed to see Maa.
I stepped into the ICU.

She was there.
Still.

I touched her cheek. Cold.
She always hated the cold.
And now she had become it.

I broke right there in the corridor.
Shattered into a thousand pieces.

I wasn't quiet.
I screamed.
I cried loud enough for the hospital walls to remember me.

I held the doctor's leg, begging, pleading, choking on my sobs.
"Please… please make my Maa like before… please…"

The world around me blurred.

The nurse nearby started crying.
A woman from the next bed held her child tighter, her face wet with silent tears.

Even strangers grieved with me — not because they knew my mother, but because pain like that doesn't need translation.

In that moment, the hospital was no longer sterile or silent.
It was soaked in sorrow.

And still — nothing changed.
I couldn't bring her back.
I couldn't fix her.
I couldn't fix anything.

Even today, whenever I pass that hospital, my chest tightens.
Not because of the building…
But because that place still holds my loudest scream.

And in that moment, I understood something no fifteen-year-old should ever have to carry.

Baba hadn't just lost his wife.
He had lost his compass. His calm. His constant.

He was the car.
But she held the wheel.

She didn't just know the roads — she memorised every turn.
She slowed down at every curve.
She carried the snacks, the songs, the laughter that filled the silence.

And we — we were just passengers.
Heads at the window, staring at the sky, trusting the journey.
Never wondering who was steering.

And now?
The engine had stopped.

The road ahead? Just silence.
No signs. No headlights.
No one left to steer.

We didn't cry at first. Not out loud.
We didn't scream or break things.
We just sat. Frozen.

Trying to convince ourselves this was just another ordinary day —
One where the sun had simply set a little early.

But deep inside, we already knew.
It wasn't just the sun.
It was our entire sky.

Just a week ago, she had chased me with a rolling pin — mock fury in her eyes, still wiping her hands on a kitchen towel. I had stacked all the saucers on top of each other, trying to be clever, and ended up breaking the entire set.

She scolded me to go to the kitchen:
"Modern girls and their modern methods!"

But by evening, we were laughing.
It was Yashoda's birthday. Just us. Just Maa's pav bhaji.
Extra butter.

And now — only silence remains.

The ache is permanent.
The helplessness is unbearable.

And I keep going back, again and again, to the one truth that tears me apart:
I couldn't do anything to change it.

🕯 The Day the Sun Set Early

She didn't leave in thunder,

No storm, no scream —

Just silence loud enough

To echo in every dream.

No goodbye written,

No promise made,

Just folded clothes,

And the scent that stayed.

She was the rhythm

To our unspoken song,

The reason the weak

Could still act strong.

Now we walk,

But something's gone from the air —

Like light without warmth,

Like a temple in prayer.

But if love could echo

Through quiet halls,

It'd sound like her bangles

Dancing on walls.

She's gone, they say —

But they don't see:

She lives in courage

She planted in me.

Chapter - 5

The Space She Left Behind

"The hardest part isn't losing someone you love; it's learning to live in the space they leave behind."

-Muna

Some days pass. Some days stay. And some… stay silently, tucked between memories and moments you never asked for.

The house looked the same, but nothing felt familiar. The air was heavier. The light was dimmer, even during the day.

The tears wouldn't stop. We were shattered — like glass hit by something too strong to name. Why couldn't I change any of this? Why wasn't she coming back? Why did she become so heartless as to leave us like this? That thought alone pierced me over and over — I can't see her again, can't hear her voice. Nothing can bring her back. We all sat in separate corners of the house, crying in silence. What had we done to deserve this punishment? Why us?

We weren't talking much. Not because we didn't want to... but because words didn't know what to say anymore.

I'd sit by the kitchen door, staring at her saree that still hung behind the curtain — unmoved, untouched — like it too was waiting for her return. The bangles near the sink had lost their song. Even the radio Baba used to play in the morning remained off.

We weren't living. We were... adjusting.

I tried to step into her shoes — waking up early, checking school bags, warming the milk, braiding my sister's hair — but her rhythm was missing in everything I did. No one said it, but I could feel it — I wasn't her. I was just her memory, trying to hold the house together.

"Every morning, I remembered how she used to wake me up — not once, but five times. Her voice was soft, patient, like a lullaby in reverse. 'Muna, wake up,' she'd whisper, gently shaking my shoulder, her fingertips always warm. I would grumble, pull the blanket tighter, pretend to sleep just a little longer — because I knew she would come again. She always did.

Now? I wake up to silence. No voice. No warmth. Just an ache. I begged God to rewind time. Let me go back. I'll get up the first time she calls, I swear. I'll eat all the vegetables without a fuss. I'll help her in the kitchen, take care of her when she's unwell, and tell her how much I love her.

Just give me one more morning. One more chance to return all the love she poured into me — spoon by spoon, tear by tear.

But that chance is gone. And this silence? It is the loudest thing I've ever known."

Baba had changed, too. He looked older, quieter. His eyes were dull, his words mumbled, like he was speaking through layers of pain. He forced a smile now and then, but even his face didn't believe in it. He'd leave for work without a word and return with tired eyes that rarely met ours. He was still our superhero — but now, even heroes looked like they needed saving.

And me? I was trying to grow up faster than I was ready for. I had SSC board exams, younger siblings, a house to run, and a grief that didn't know how to leave.

Some nights, I'd stare at the ceiling, whispering her name in the dark. "Where are you, Maa? Can you still see us? Are you proud of me?"

I kept wishing she'd reply — even just once — through a dream, a breeze, a whisper in the dark. But nothing came.

And in those moments, I didn't cry loudly. I just… blinked slower. Because sometimes, even crying felt like it would break whatever was left holding me together.

I would cover my face with the pillow, trying not to let anyone hear me. The world expected me to move on, but I hadn't even taken the first step. Every inch of the house reminded me of her — every corner echoed her absence.

Grief doesn't ask you if you're ready. It just hands you a new life — and walks away.

Some days, we managed — thanks to my Buva and her daughter, Sapana Didi. They stepped in, stood by us like steady walls during an earthquake. For that, I'll always be grateful. But even then, I knew — no one can hold your house forever. At some point, you must stand up and pick up the broken bricks yourself.

Carrying Her Dreams Forward

It had been four months since Maa was gone. One evening, I came back from tuition and saw Baba sitting in the corner of the sofa, looking at Maa's photo, eyes lost, expression frozen. That photo had become both his anchor and his wound. I called out to him softly, "Baba..." He sat frozen, unreachable — as if my voice was just an echo in a world he no longer understood. I walked closer and said again, "Baba, I'll leave school… I can handle both — the house and my studies. Though honestly, I can't even focus right now. I keep missing Maa."

He looked up at me, his eyes red and wet. I saw something I had never seen before — Baba crying. He quickly wiped his tears, took a deep breath, and said softly, "Haa, Nani..."

That one word — Nani — carried a lifetime of love and ache.

He held my hand, as if drawing strength from it, and said, "You misunderstood your Maa. She didn't want you to give up. She wanted you to rise. If she could speak now, she'd say — go, study, fly… make us proud. Don't stop, beta. Not now."

That day, my decision changed.

So, I gathered myself. Held back my tears. And began waking up at 5 a.m., just like she did.

Some mornings, the rice was undercooked. Some days, the dal was too salty. Other times, the food was spicy enough to make eyes water — but no one complained.

We were learning. Stumbling. But trying.

Pima — just 13 — washed clothes and utensils with her bare, tiny hands. Scrubbing, scrubbing, scrubbing like she was trying to clean away the grief itself. Her knuckles would turn red, her small back bent over cold buckets of water. Sometimes she'd hum softly — maybe to distract herself, maybe to remember Maa. But even the songs felt unfinished. Her childhood was slipping away, wash by wash.

Yashoda, who should've been playing with dolls, now held a broom taller than her.. She dusted the same shelves where Maa used to place her bangles — tiny echoes of glass still clung to the corners. Her hands, meant for crayons and storybooks, grew rough with chores far too big for her little fingers. She didn't complain. She just watched. Silently learning how to fill a space too wide for her age.

And Vishnu — he changed in a way that broke something in me. No more tantrums over broken toys. No more jumping at the sound of the ice cream cart. He would just sit cross-legged in front of Maa's photo, his small eyes locked onto hers. Not crying.

Not blinking. Just… waiting.

I used to wonder what he saw there — what he was searching for in that still frame.

Were they answers? Was it the sound of her voice? Or maybe the quiet miracle of her walking back through the door, smiling like before.

He never said a word. But in his silence, I heard everything — the questions, the ache, the hope that refused to die.

It wasn't just me who was hurting. I realised — it was all of us. We were each breaking in our own quiet corners, sharing the same storm, but hiding it from each other. Pretending to be strong, just so the others wouldn't shatter.. It wasn't just me who was trying to grow up too soon. My whole family was bleeding — emotionally and physically.

Baba, silently holding the weight of it all, developed high blood pressure. Stress carved lines into his face that even age hadn't touched. At night, I'd hear his muffled sobs behind the bathroom door. By morning, he'd wipe his face clean and walk out like everything was okay. But we saw it — the superhero mask was cracking.

And Dajyu… he stayed the same. Maa had always treated him like her prince. She never gave him responsibilities, and after she was gone, nothing changed. Maybe grief froze him differently. Maybe he didn't know how to step in. But it felt like we lost two people that day — Maa and the brother.

Loss had reshaped our family — Baba's stoicism, Dajyu's detachment, and the unspoken burden that now fell on the youngest among us.

I still remember the emptiness of that evening — the house looked the same, but her absence made every small task feel like a mountain, and every hungry child a reminder of what we had lost.

It was a regular school evening, maybe more tiring than usual. Around 5:30 p.m., I dragged myself home — my uniform sticking to me, soaked in sweat and exhaustion, my back aching under the weight of books and burdens. As I entered, expecting the usual silence, I saw them — Yashoda and Vishnu — sitting quietly by the door, their legs folded, their eyes heavy.

"Didi… we're hungry."

My heart sank.

We had run out of food. No one had eaten lunch.

Without a word, I dropped my bag. Didn't even change. I grabbed the leftover rice, vegetables and quickly made khichdi. Simple. Warm. Comforting.

They ate with such joy… like it was a feast.

That night, I cried into my pillow. Not loudly. But deep… like it came from somewhere ancient inside me.

Oh, God, why is this happening to us? What sin have we committed? What wrong did Baba do? Why must my little siblings bear this unbearable burden of sorrow?

Why was our laughter and joy snatched away so abruptly, leaving us in the shadow of grief? Why was our happiness extinguished so early, so cruelly, so unexpectedly?

But there was no reply. Just silence. And the weight of growing up too soon.

Still, the story wasn't over. Not yet.

Yashoda got her first period, and she did not understand what was happening. She stood there, scared and confused, and asked, "Didi, what is this?" She needed her mother for comfort and guidance. I tried to help her, but I was not her mother. No matter how tightly I hugged her, Yashoda kept looking around, searching for the one who would never come back.

Vishnu's grades started to drop, and he failed an exam. Maa had been his tutor. She spent every afternoon and evening with him, providing gentle encouragement and patience. Now that she was gone, he felt lost. We couldn't afford a tutor, and both Dajyu, who was in 12th grade, and I, in 10th grade, needed help. I struggled to keep up with my own studies.

At school, I was physically present, but my mind was elsewhere, tangled in a web of home worries. Had the food I made been enough for everyone? What should I cook today? I hope Yashoda doesn't touch the gas switches… Is Baba managing okay? I tried to juggle schedules, schoolwork, and the constant hum of responsibility. It felt like too much for anyone, yet I had to keep going.

Eventually, my health began to suffer. I felt tired and overwhelmed, unable to cope with all the responsibilities and stress. Fainting spells. Fever every night. A strange ache in my chest. Hands that wouldn't stop shivering. Skin turning yellow.

More tests. More fear.

Tuberculosis. Every breath is a battle. Baba didn't cry, but his eyes told the story—same fear as the day Maa left us. Afraid of losing me, too. The younger ones clung tight, tiny hands gripping, silent prayers in their wide, worried eyes.

I was eating more medicines than food.

While other girls my age dreamed of the spicy crunch of pani puri and the creamy delight of ice cream, my meals consisted solely of bitter pills and lukewarm water, lacking flavour and joy.

At just 15, an age filled with hopes and dreams, I felt much older, like I was dragging a weary body that seemed to take forever to heal.

Yet, even in this challenging time, my dreams stayed alive, refusing to be buried beneath the weight of illness.

I wanted to wear those shiny red high heels. Walk into the office lobby like a warrior in disguise. Make Maa proud — wherever she was.

A Letter to Life.

Help came when Mrs. Kamble, our caring school principal, noticed my struggle behind my smile. She called my teachers together and said,

"No child should suffer for what life has taken from her."

They responded by offering me extra classes for free, without any conditions—just a kind gesture.

With this support, I started to heal. I found the strength to pick up my books and return to my studies. Then came the day of my first board exam.

I can still vividly recall the day my elder brother was set to take his 10th-grade exams. Our mother, in her unwavering faith, fasted and prayed all day long, her hands clasped tightly in devotion as she devoted herself to his success.

And then there was me.

I found myself standing in front of her framed photograph, the familiar yet haunting image of her gentle smile, feeling an overwhelming sense of solitude. I whispered a prayer, my fingers trembling slightly as I wiped away the tears that had silently rolled down my cheeks. With a deep breath, I slung my bag over my shoulder—a familiar weight that seemed heavier that day.

As I approached the school gate, I could hear the jubilant sounds of other parents. They clapped enthusiastically, showering their children with kisses and blessings, their faces alight with pride and encouragement.

And there I was—

Walking through the gate quietly, blending into the background. No cheers echoed around me, no joyous send-off from a parent. Just a girl, carrying the weight of her aspirations on one shoulder and the quiet burden of her world on the other, determined to forge her path against all odds. My hands held more than just a pen that day. They held promises. They held pain. They held the silent strength of a girl becoming a woman… far too soon.

That day, I didn't just write an exam — I wrote a quiet, unspoken letter to life itself:

I was hoping you could take what you must, but you won't take my fire. I will rise through the ache, build hope from the mire. I'll wear her dreams on tired feet, walk roads she prayed I'd find, and carry forward every whisper Maa left behind.

Carrying Her Light

Rooms are quiet, yet full of sound,

Small hands are busy, hearts unbound.

Through empty spaces, her whispers stay,

Guiding our steps along the day.

Her laughter lingers in the air,

A gentle echo everywhere.

We stumble, we rise, we learn to cope,

Holding on to threads of hope.

Bitter pills and sleepless nights,

Tired eyes chasing distant lights.

Yet in our hearts, her love remains—

A steady fire through all our pains.

Chapter - 6

A Second Nest, A Softer Sky

"They say time heals everything. But no one tells you what to do when time moves on, and the pain stays behind."

It doesn't scream anymore—it hums. A quiet wound, stitched into the fabric of everyday.

I've stopped trying to erase it. Now I just… live with it. Like a bird that knows its wings will never be the same, but flies anyway.

For a long time, the pain stayed curled around me like an old sweater—the kind that scratches your skin, but you can't take off because it's all you have. Everywhere I looked, I saw mothers fixing their daughters' sarees, waiting outside tuitions, scolding them over phone calls. I'd catch myself watching for too long. Trying to memorise how a girl leaned on her mother's shoulder, or how a mother smiled with her whole face. Then I'd quickly look away, like I had seen something sacred I wasn't allowed to touch.

If I saw an old lady walking with her daughter, I'd whisper to God: "Why us? Why not her?"

It wasn't that I wished loss upon anyone—I just wanted to understand why ours came so soon. So suddenly. Without mercy or pause. Everyone else got a full story. I got a torn page.

Baba said yes

One day, I overheard my grandparents talking to Baba. They weren't asking him to remarry for himself—they were thinking of us. "Who will take care of the kids?" "You go to work all day—they need someone." "You still have a whole life ahead of you. How will you live it alone?" "One day, they'll grow up and leave. And we won't always be around."

And then Baba said yes—not softly, but under pressure. A reluctant, tired, yes, that felt more like surrender than choice.

The only word that echoed in my head was: Stepmother. That word felt like a throne made of roses… with thorns tucked underneath.

I didn't know what stepmothers were like in real life—but in Bollywood, they were villains. I had seen Lalita Pawar's arched eyebrows. Heard the dramatic background music. Watched as the poor girl was locked in rooms, fed stale leftovers while her siblings had paneer.

So, when Baba said he would remarry, I saw all the warning signs—flashing, underlined, with music in my head. I didn't want her. I didn't want anyone. I just wanted Maa back.

Even the kindest woman wouldn't pass the test I wasn't ready to give.

The day she entered our home, I didn't greet her. I went straight into Maa's room and cried into her old saree. I didn't care if it made sense or not—I felt betrayed. Like Baba had moved on before I could even catch my breath. Like this woman would change everything. Like she'd erase the last traces of Maa still echoing in our walls.

My grandparents tried to console me, but their words felt like knives, not comfort. Each sentence, meant to soothe, instead felt like it was cutting away the space Maa had left behind. I heard her soft footsteps. I felt her presence. But I stayed hidden. I wasn't ready. Not yet.

Filling the Unseen Spaces

I didn't speak to her for months. Not a word. But silence didn't stop her. She quietly began to take responsibility, waking up early, managing meals, and checking on our health. Without expectation. Without complaint. She did what needed to be done—not to win us over, but because someone had to keep us going.

Slowly, things began to shift. She didn't try to wear my mother's shadow. She didn't arrive with promises or rehearsed affection. She was the woman who waited at the door until we were ready to let her in. Not to replace the one we lost—but to remind us that we could be loved again, in a different way, by a different kind of softness.

She began noticing our likes and dislikes—my brother's favourite vegetable, my sister's allergy, and my missed medicines. She sat by me on days I couldn't get out of bed. And one day, without even realising it, I was talking to her like a friend—sharing school stories, secrets, frustrations.

Our bond didn't come with grand declarations. It arrived like quiet rain after a long drought. Built in burnt rotis, shared silences, and the comfort of knowing someone was there.

She never asked us to call her Maa, Mumma or Aama. And I couldn't. That name belonged to the woman whose bangles still echoed in the walls. But this woman didn't ask for her place. She built her own.

We gave her a name of our own: Chama—aunty. Not quite a mother. Not just a stranger. Just… her. A new bond. A new name. Born from quiet presence, not blood. She smiled the first time we said it, and in that smile, I saw something I hadn't seen in a long time: understanding. Years later, when we were grown, we realized she had given us all the love she possibly could. Slowly, without asking, without demanding — Chama had become our Aama.

She never spoke much about her past, but one day, she did. Slowly, quietly, she told me about the years of domestic violence she had endured. Her Ex husband—a drunkard and a cheater—didn't just break her heart; he shattered her spirit. She had two sons. One was taken by him, and the other, Sujan, just five years old, was left with her. Choosing to remarry wasn't easy. It wasn't a second chance—it was her only chance at rebuilding what life had stolen.

Fitting Into Us

A few months later, Baba brought Sujan home. He said, "What is that child's fault? Why should he stay in his aunt's house when he has a family?"

Sujan came with soft eyes and small hands. He didn't ask for much—just a little love. And that little boy, without even knowing it, began to win hearts. He tried hard to impress us with his obedience, his silly jokes, his need to belong. He used to call us whenever we were late, checking if we were safe. He was trying hard to be a family. Somehow, he impressed all of us. Even today, when I need help, he's the first one I call. My respect for Baba—and for her—only grew after that.

10th March

Aama and I shared the same birthday on 10th March—an odd, almost divine coincidence that always felt like a quiet wink from the universe. One year, I took out one of Maa's old sarees — a soft blue and black one she wore often, the kind that still carried her scent and memories. I didn't wrap it. I folded it the way Maa used to after laundry days, every crease a habit I had memorised, and placed it gently in Aama's hands. She didn't say much. Just ran her fingers across it like it was something sacred. Maybe she knew — it wasn't just a saree. It was an unspoken offering. A bridge. A whisper that said, 'I see you. And I'm trying.'

That night, as I folded the empty saree cover and placed it back, I realised — sometimes, family isn't something you are born into. Sometimes, it's something you choose to accept, one memory at a time.

That saree didn't just bridge our past—it welcomed a new presence into it. After that day, something shifted. She didn't feel like a guest anymore. She felt like part of the air we breathed.

And now, when I look back, I wonder if she was sent by someone above—not to fill the space Maa left, but to sit gently beside it and help us live again. It wasn't just me who was healing—we were all learning to share our grief, to talk about it, and eventually, to smile again. Slowly, the house started breathing again. Laughter returned—quietly at first, like a guest unsure of its welcome—and then louder, like it remembered where it belonged.

I also saw Baba—doing his best in silence. Sometimes, he acted distant with Aama. Not because he was rude, but maybe because he thought if he gave her too much importance, we'd feel insecure. That's how he protected us—not with words, but with space. Maybe he didn't know how to balance love and loyalty. Maybe none of us did. But we were all learning—in our own, awkward, human ways.

With her help, I began to heal

Not just physically, but emotionally. For the first time in years, I could focus on myself again. Because Aama took all the burdens and told me gently, "You focus on your studies. Let me handle the rest."

And she meant it. From daily chores to doctor appointments, she quietly held the house together—giving me the gift of time, of clarity, of breath. She didn't push me to move on; she simply created a space where I could move forward—without guilt.

In her silence, I found steadiness. In her presence, I found the freedom to dream again.

SSC Result

Just as we began to breathe easier, my SSC results were about to be declared. It was 2005, and you could now check your results online. Because of everything—Maa's sudden passing, our emotional breakdown, my illness—Baba had no expectations. He just prayed I'd pass. That was enough for him.

He requested one of his seniors at work to check my result. He was sure I hadn't made it. He had seen my struggle too closely. But when his boss called out the number—69.63%—Baba's face lit up. He couldn't believe it. He came home with sweets in his hand and pride in his eyes. It wasn't a great score by academic standards—but for him, it was more than enough. Because he thought I would fail. And I didn't.

Even my teachers and principal were prouder of me than of those who had scored higher—because they knew what I had survived. That joy, however, was short-lived. The world doesn't pause just because you've survived something.

College admissions began—and so did the next set of struggles. I wanted to pursue science. But with my percentage, my name didn't appear on any merit list. And if your name wasn't on the list, you had to pay heavy admission fees—something we simply couldn't afford.

That dream—like many before—had to be let go. It hurt, but not as deeply as before. Maybe because this time, I understood: some dreams bend to make space for others.

So, I took admission in commerce.

And yet again, a new world opened—one that scared me. The college crowd. Everyone spoke in English. Teachers taught in English. It all felt so polished, so fast, so far from the world I came from. I had studied in the Marathi medium. I knew English, yes—but not the kind that flowed effortlessly in classrooms and corridors.

But I didn't back down. I worked hard. Took notes. Watched, listened, learned. And by the end of the year, something amazing happened—I was not only coping, I was helping others. I was teaching my friends Accounts. I had become the topper in Accounts.

This victory wasn't just mine. It belonged to Aama, who had recently come into our lives and already given so much. She had taken the burden, so I could build the future. She created the quiet, so I could find my voice. Because of her, I could rise—not just as a student, but as a girl who was slowly remembering how to dream.

She didn't just help me pass—she helped me begin again. And like a bird with wounded wings, I wasn't just flying—I was learning the sky all over again.

And in this second nest, under this softer sky, I began to feel the sun again.

A Softer Sky

I stitched my wounds with quiet thread,

And rose from nights I thought I'd dread.

Not in leaps, but little tries,

Not in noise — but softened skies.

She held the roof when rain came fast,

She didn't erase — she stood beside the past.

In borrowed strength, I learned to stand,

To dream again, with open hand.

So here I am — not whole, but free,

Not who I was… but still, fully me.

Chapter - 7

Salaam Namaste to Myself

"Life doesn't give you the script — just the stage. And sometimes, you forget your lines, trip on your heels, and still have to keep performing."

Life isn't linear. It doesn't move in straight, neat lines. It zigzags, stumbles, loops back, and sometimes feels like it's laughing at your plans. Just when you think you've settled into the rhythm, it changes the music. And yet — we dance. Even when we don't know the steps.

I had scored decent marks in 12th. But dreams don't survive on marks alone — they need money. And I had already buried one dream — to become a doctor. Left it behind without a fight, because the fees were too high and our pain was already expensive. I didn't cry that day. I just looked away, as if even dreaming had become a luxury.

When it was time to choose a course, I looked at B.Com. It was simple. Affordable. Practical. And I was ready to compromise again.

But Baba wasn't. He had seen enough sacrifices. This time, he wanted a win — for me, and maybe for the version of himself that once dreamed of becoming a journalist.

He looked at me one evening, while sipping his tea, and said with a quiet grin: "One day, my daughter will become a journalist so powerful, even the truth will pause when she speaks — and the corrupt will tremble."

To him, journalism wasn't just a profession — it was a weapon against injustice, a spotlight that could expose lies, a pen that could rewrite fates. It meant being the voice for those unheard, the eyes for those blindfolded by power. It was about asking the right questions when everyone else stayed silent, about shining light where others saw only darkness. Journalism, he believed, could shape societies, shake governments, and stir revolutions—all with truth and courage inked into every line. And in his belief, I saw something bigger than a career—I saw a chance to change the world with words.

I laughed, trying to brush it off — but he didn't. He meant every word. He quietly took a loan. Filled out my BMM admission form like he was filling his own. Stood beside me at the counter, watching every word on the paper like it was sacred.

That day, he didn't just pay my fees — he handed me a torch. Lit with belief. Fueled by hope. And just like that, BMM wasn't just a degree. It was a promise. A shared dream between a daughter and her Baba. And this time, I vowed — I wouldn't let it go.

The College, The Dreams, and The Mic

Stepping into my new college felt like stepping into a movie set. The campus was massive, with tall buildings that echoed ambition, a sports ground lined with white railings, and curated gardens that looked like they were arranged by a perfectionist florist. The main building had wide stairs that felt like they belonged to someone important, and I remember running my hand along the cool railing, half-expecting background music to play. For a girl who had mostly lived in small houses and borrowed dreams, this place felt too polished, too distant. And yet, I was excited. A new beginning. A new chapter. But alongside the thrill was a quiet fear.

Because inside those impressive walls were students who spoke fluent English. And that was intimidating. My English was basic — polite enough to survive, but not enough to speak in a room full of strangers.

And then came Ex-tempore. We had to introduce ourselves, share our hobbies, and speak for five minutes on a surprise topic. Simple, right?

Except… the auditorium was packed. About 150 students. Confident laughter — the kind that makes your insecurities scream louder. I held the mic like it was a lifeline. Took a deep breath.

"Hi… my name is…"

And then — blank. The one word I've heard every day since birth — gone. Blank screen. Cursor blinking. Zero input. My brain didn't just freeze — it evacuated. I forgot my own name.

Someone from the crowd shouted, “Skip the intro! Just speak on the topic!” They handed me a chit.

Topic: Live-in Relationship.

Live in what? Live-in where? With whom? My thoughts tangled like headphones in a pocket. I was from a home where even two actors hugging in a TV serial meant someone would immediately change the channel.

Another student laughed, “Just talk about Salaam Namaste!”

Honestly, I thought 'live-in' meant something like PG accommodation… with a friendship bonus. Maybe like being roommates… but with feelings?

So, I said the only thing my poor, fried brain could come up with:

"Uh… live-in relationship means… you live in… and… you relate."

Silence. You could hear the fan creaking.

Then — snorts. And finally, loud, unfiltered laughter.

I stood there like a weak Wi-Fi signal — connected, but nothing was loading.

Someone kindly changed the topic: “Anti-smoking.”

I cleared my throat, straightened up, and delivered my profound TED Talk: "Smoking is injurious to health."

My voice trembled like a loose mic wire. I wiped the sweat from my forehead, hoping no one would notice how badly my hands were shaking. Then I added, with all the genius I had left: "Smoking is bad… because it’s injurious to health."

That's it. No stats. No emotion. Not even a fake cough for effect. The teacher gave me the "okay, dear, next time" smile. The students chuckled. And I walked out — not just embarrassed, but shattered.

At that moment, I didn't want applause. I wanted invisibility. I wish I could live-in silence.

And just like that, the laughter faded — leaving behind a silence louder than the mic feedback.

That evening, and for many nights after, I kept replaying the moment in my head. But in my dreams, I stood on that same stage — this time not scared, but shining. I wore heels. People clapped. I smiled.

As I lay there imagining the version of me I wanted to become, my mind drifted to something unexpected — a childhood memory. A small summer moment that had somehow waited silently for this very day.

I was around ten, and Baba had brought home a slim storybook during summer vacation. One of those moral tales, filled with talking animals and divine interventions.

In it, a poor, humble man — loyal and sincere, and a big devotee of Lord Shiva—is visited by God, impressed by his unwavering devotion. Every day, despite hunger and hardship, the man prayed with sincerity, helped others, and never walked the wrong path, even when temptation knocked loudly. He struggled, yet remained kind. He had nothing, yet never complained.

Moved by his unshaken faith and honesty in a world full of shortcuts, Lord Shiva appears before him.

“I’ll grant you one wish,” Lord Shiva says. “Anything you ask.”

The man asks for one night to think about it. He spends the entire night imagining it all: a big house, gold, jewellery, endless food, the riches he’d never known. But the next morning, he joined his hands and says, "Lord, give me self-confidence."

At ten, I had rolled my eyes. What a waste! I thought. He could’ve had anything. And he chose that?

But that day, when I forgot my name in a packed auditorium, I finally understood.

It wasn’t about knowledge. It wasn’t about language. It was about confidence.

Because you don’t forget your name out of ignorance — you forget it when you no longer trust your voice to speak it out loud.

That moment on stage wasn’t just stage fright. It was the weight of every judging face, every silent giggle, every voice in my head whispering, "You’re not good enough."

Real, true self-confidence is important. When you don’t believe in yourself, you can’t access what you already know. You hesitate. You freeze. And slowly, you start outsourcing your choices, your opinions, your voice, to the world around you. And that’s dangerous. Because then, your life becomes everyone’s decision but yours.

That man in the story wasn’t foolish. He was wise — decades ahead of me.

Because with self-confidence, you don’t just speak. You are heard.

When They Laughed, I Listened

They laughed when I froze on stage,

When my words hid behind fear.

They saw a girl with trembling hands —

Not the battles she fought each year.

They didn't hear the silent voice,

Or late-night, tear-stained lines.

They never saw her stitch her soul.

With metaphors and rhymes.

They mocked the silence in her speech,

The pauses in her name —

But missed the spark behind her eyes.

That quietly fed the flame.

She found her voice between the cracks,

In poems that knew her pain.

And in each word, she dared to write,

She learned to breathe again.

Chapter - 8

"Echoes of the Unspoken"

"You don't grow when you speak loudly. You grow when you speak, even when your voice shakes."

— ***Muna***

The first time I lost my voice, I wasn't sick — I was scared. And fear, I learned, can be louder than any crowd.

The mic slipped from my trembling hands, but the silence didn't end there. It followed me home, crept into my dreams, and sat beside me like a cold shadow. That moment on stage — forgetting my name, my voice, my whole self — didn't just pass. It left a bruise I could feel deep in my bones.

And yet, within that bruise, something else began to grow. Not loudly, but quietly — a stubborn, fragile dream. I saw a version of myself, years later, standing on a stage, speaking like I belonged there. I didn't know how to become her, but I knew I wanted to.

I would learn much later that confidence isn't about knowing everything — it's about trusting that what you know is enough to begin. Back then, I had only one question: *How do I become her? Where do I start?*

The answer didn't come quickly. But the questions stayed. And so did the dream.

Maybe that whisper inside me wasn't born that day at all. Maybe it had been waiting for years — since the night I wrote my first poem.

The Woman Who Showed Me More

"Start reading. It will help."

The advice came from **Srija Chechi** — our neighbour, our guide, our quiet anchor. Wrapped in soft cotton sarees, she was like our Google, our protector, and our comfort. When we had no family nearby, she stood by us as if she'd always been ours.

When I passed my exams, she gifted me a red-and-yellow suit — bold and bright, like her blessings. When I was lost, she fed me idlis and understanding. Her food didn't just warm my body; it healed my spirit.

She taught me to drape a saree neatly, to grind coconut chutney just right, to pronounce tricky English words — always with kindness, never mockery. She didn't just give advice; she handed me tools for life.

When I told her about my speech disaster, she smiled with that quiet wisdom and said simply, "Start reading. It will help."

So, I read — old newspapers, TV subtitles, traffic signs, even shampoo bottles in the bathroom. Not because I loved words yet, but because I was searching for my own.

The First Poem: A Quiet Breakthrough

In my second year of college, we had a Creative Writing class. Our teacher handed us a list of rhyming words and said, "Write a poem."

I froze. Me? The girl who still stumbled over her own name during roll call?

Still, something inside nudged me forward. Ten pages of scribbling, scratching out, and rewriting later, I had my first piece:

My Life

Today, I want to cry —

But I don't know why.

My life feels like a wounded bird,

Too tired to sing, too hurt for words.

I see others flying high,

And wonder, without joy —

Can I even try?

I want to see the morning light,

But I'm lost in the arms of night.

Still, if someday I find that ray,

I'll rise and wipe the dark away.

And I'll say —

I want to try.

I want to try.

It wasn't perfect. But it was honest. And for the first time, I didn't feel judged. I felt heard — even if only by the paper and my own shaky heart.

That night, I slept peacefully, as if the page had carried away some of my pain. I didn't know it then, but I had found my way of speaking, even when my voice couldn't. From that moment, whenever life was too loud or too unfair, I didn't shout. I wrote. My poems became my refuge, my voice, my silent, unshakable act of defiance.

From Pain to Performance: Finding My Reason

One day, my friends and I joined a group called *Media Matters*. Our first meeting was about female feticide. The facts hit me hard. They weren't just numbers — they were stolen stories, lives that never got to be.

Moved by this injustice, we wrote a play: *Main Aasha*. Each of us played Asha at different moments in her short life. This wasn't just acting; it was purpose.

We didn't perform in big halls. We went where silence was heavier — village schools, orphanages, old age homes, rehabitation centre. They watched us closely. We watched them. And something deep shifted — not just in them, but in us too.

After meeting people who had faced far worse, I stopped seeing myself as the saddest story in the room. Their quiet bravery became my mirror. It reflected not pity, but deep strength — and it became my guide.

Where Dreams Found Their Way In

My degree in BMM wasn't just a certificate. It was the road where I began discovering who I was becoming. I wasn't just surviving anymore — I was reaching, growing, aiming higher.

Then came the Mumbai Marathon. Five days of volunteering, handing out numbers. A simple job — but in that sea of people stood John Abraham. Not on a poster, but right there in front of me.

It lit a spark. I didn't just want to see stars; I wanted to become one.

So, I kept showing up — every event, every odd shift, no matter the hours. There was no glamour, no spotlight, just work. But with each shift, I learned: how to speak clearly, how to stay calm in chaos, how to stand my ground. Without realising it, I was chiselling away at my fears.

More Than My Struggles

The girl who once forgot her name on stage was now organising things backstage. Helping volunteers. Managing artists. Running the whole show from behind the curtains.

The fear hadn't disappeared — but now, it fueled me. It became my engine, not my brake.

I stopped comparing my clothes, my English, and my accent to others. I had found something far more precious inside: grit, drive, and dreams that refused to quit.

College wasn't just educating me. It was shaping me, day by day, into someone I never imagined I could be — someone who could lead without shouting, who could fall and rise again without needing applause.

I no longer needed the world's claps. I had my own — echoing strongly from within.

I wasn't just the girl with scars anymore. I was the bird that flies — not despite the pain, but because of it.

It's the wind against broken wings that truly teaches you how to fly your own special way. My story wasn't about hiding the scars. It was about flying with them — bravely, openly.

And finally, I had started to soar.

Chapter - 9

The Girl Gang — Who Made the Storm Feel Like Spring

(The Chapter I Never Wanted to End)

They say college is where you find your career. I say — it's where I found a kind of home I didn't know I needed. A home made of late-night chai, emergency hugs, and five cups of absolute chaos.

My girl gang. My beautiful, unpredictable circus.

Looking back, it feels like a dream I can still almost touch.

Five Cups of Madness

We were five — wildly different, stubbornly bonded, and just the right amount of mad. Each of us was a one-woman show. Together? A full-blown, award-winning drama.

Jyoti — Jo to us — beautiful, confident, always three steps ahead in syllabus and skincare. A multitasking queen who could pull off red lipstick and a last-minute pitch with the same flair. She moisturised with passion and submitted projects on time — often ours too.

Pavitra — Pavi — feminist, fierce, and the unofficial first-aid expert for every ailment. If you sneezed, she had both a theory and a remedy. She wore specs like a crown and loved with the gentleness of coconut malai — soft, rare, nurturing. But mess with her people? She'd burn the whole world down with you inside it.

Rameshwari — Ramu — a quiet storm with a camera and a head full of philosophical confusion. Focused, floaty, full of feelings. She got mad only at people she loved — which meant she was always yelling at us. Her anger was oddly comforting, like Mumbai rain — loud, messy, and honest.

Dipti — our confused cupcake. Left-handed, with romantic-novel handwriting and big button eyes. She didn't talk much, but her eyebrows could perform a whole Bollywood scene. She sipped chai only after it cooled — possibly the only human in existence to do so.

And then there was me — the dreamer with borrowed confidence. Sarcastic on the outside, soft on the inside. The "ideal daughter" at everyone's house. Their parents loved me. But my gang saw through the act. They sensed the part of me that stayed quiet, that held things in like it was my job.

Pavi took this as a personal challenge.

"Speak up, Muna! Why are you a mute spectator in your own life?"

I'd laugh and say, "Because you're shouting enough for both of us."

Back then, it was just a joke. Now I know — that was me protecting my silence. And they, gently breaking through it.

Project Nights, Branding Fights & the Birth of 'Shringar'

College projects were like distant relatives — they arrived uninvited, overstayed, and brought more drama than value.

Everyone had laptops and Wi-Fi. I had a second-hand pen drive and zero storage — emotionally and digitally.

So, we declared Ramu's house as HQ:

One desktop. Endless chai. Guaranteed chaos.

Our ritual:

- 10 minutes of actual work
- 1 hour of distractions
- 4 hours of gossip
- One dramatic breakdown

I was the official chai-wali. If not academically useful, I could at least caffeinate. Sometimes I'd nap, and Jo would say, "Muna, we finished your part." I'd make extra tea in apology.

Then came our masterpiece project — Branding.

Other groups got yoga kits and fitness trackers.

We got... hair removal cream.

Even feminism took a moment of silence.

We looked at each other like someone had cursed our career paths. Then Pavi, voice like thunder, said:

“Of all the cool products in the world, we got this... blessing.”

We burst into laughter. Crying felt dramatic. Quitting felt illegal.

So, we embraced our fate — with sarcasm, snacks, and collective delusion.

Brainstorming began:

“Hair Today, Gone Tomorrow.”

“Velvet Touch.”

“Slick Retreat.”

At 3 a.m., someone whispered, “Shringar — the 17th modern need of beauty.” It stuck. A sleepy whisper turned into a legend.

I pitched the concept for our ad — a funny, low-budget TVC shot on a rented camcorder. Phones back then didn’t have cameras. Just Snake and missed calls.

Jo directed like a dictator.

Pavi modelled under protest.

Dipti handled makeup like a Bollywood artist.

Ramu filmed like she was covering wildlife.

We wore black sarees and fake confidence like armour.

Our tagline?

"Hair removal. Pain removal. Stress removal — all in one swipe."

The ad was a hit. Not just a submission — a shared memory. One that still lives in the group chat.

Movie Magic: Jaane Tu... Ya Jaane Na

One lazy afternoon, during a cancelled lecture, Jo stood up and announced, "I am bored, let's go watch a movie."

We blinked. "Suddenly? What happened?"

She shrugged. "Don't think so much. Let's go!"

Just like that, ₹410 was pooled like a national budget:

- Jo: ₹100
- Ramu: ₹100
- Me: ₹50
- Pavi: ₹80
- Dipti: ₹80

Tickets: ₹350. Leftover: ₹60 — one water bottle and five samosas. Nutrition? Achieved.

The movie? *Jaane Tu... Ya Jaane Na* — a story of friendship, love, and growing up with your gang. We didn't just watch it — we lived it.

Dipti sobbed.

Jo hummed the songs on the train.

Ramu whispered under a rainy shade, “Let’s never get married. Let’s live together. Work, travel, chill.”

We all nodded like revolutionaries.

“No boys. No drama. Just pyjama.”

A wild plan. A soft promise. Stitched into soda-stained sleeves and oily notebooks. And for a moment, it felt like enough to survive the world.

Rain, Exams & Emotional Meltdowns

By the fifth semester, the Mumbai monsoon had lost its mind.

One day, returning from an exam — drenched and defeated — the trains stopped. Rickshaws vanished. So we walked to Jo’s house — soaked, tired, and buzzing.

We reached Jo’s house after two hours — a journey that usually took fifteen minutes. Soaked, shivering, and half-limping, we looked like laundry abandoned mid-wash. The rain had been merciless. Even our umbrellas had surrendered — flipped inside out like bad decisions.

Jo’s mom opened the door and gasped like it was a daily soap.

“Oh my god, come in! You girls will catch Cold!”

She wrapped us in towels, handed out dry clothes, and served hot food with that unmatched Bollywood Maa energy. Within minutes, we transformed from drowned rats to mildly presentable students.

We were supposed to study for next day’s exam — subject: Copywriting.

We opened the books with good intentions. Truly.

But our bodies had other plans

Heavy eyelids. Stiff fingers. Blank minds.

And outside, the world looked like a scene straight out of a horror film. Lightning danced across the sky. The clouds growled. Through Jo's window, we could see the railway station — empty tracks, flickering lights, water rising like plot tension.

Jo stared out at the lashing rain and said the most beautiful lie we wanted to hear: "I don't think trains will run. They'll cancel the exam."

Silence.

In Mumbai, that kind of monsoon was the magical signal for a sudden holiday and a canceled exam

Five sleepy souls nodded in agreement — no fact-checking, no news, no logic. Just blind hope wrapped in blankets.

We tossed the books aside and slid under one thick rajai.

And just like that, we dozed off like it was a holiday.

Because believing in that lie was warmer than any study plan.

At 5 a.m., Jo shot up like a haunted soul and started waking us one by one. Nobody responded. She screamed: "Sky's clear. Trains are running!"

Cue: panic.

"You said the exam would be cancelled!"

"I thought it would be!"

"What now?!"

"READ ANYTHING!"

We scrambled. Someone thought copywriting meant copying. I read jingles backwards. And still, we gave the exam.

One question:

Write a radio jingle for toothpaste.

My answer:

"Clean like never before — with detergent power and maa ka pyaar!"

Sleep-deprived? Yes. Regretful? Not at all.

Jo had a talent — post every exam, she gave Oscar-level meltdowns.

"I'm FAILING! I didn't even write the conclusion!"

Cue the tears. The dramatic gasps. The slow-motion wall slide. We, her loyal co-stars, offered water, tissues, and unsolicited pep talks.

And then — the results came.

She topped. Among us. Again.

The rest of us stood frozen, like unpaid extras in the climax of her victory film — confused and betrayed.

Pocket Money, Pocket Dreams

To earn extra cash, we worked every college fest and chaotic event. No salary — just lunch and "experience."

But oh, what experience.

We learned:

- How to walk in heels
- Smile through rude guests
- Make anchor announcements
- Guide celebrities (okay, just to the green room — but still)

We weren't rich in money, but we were wealthy in madness, Maggi, and memories.

Back Then, Now, Always

Today?

But now, life has its own punchlines.

Jo — the girl who never stepped into the kitchen — cooks full meals for her family while balancing her job and home like a pro.

Pavi — once the queen of comebacks — now says sorry before anyone even asks.

Dipti — who always blew on her cup forever — drinks her chai piping hot.

And Rameshwari? She still overthinks and confuses herself into circles. Some things never change.

And me? I still smile when they tease me.

“Hope you don’t mind, Muna...” They’d poke fun all day, then end with that line like a disclaimer.

Now I know — that was their love language.

Every laugh, every fight, every sleepless night stitched a quiet kind of love I still carry. The kind that holds you even from miles away.

Some friends are like chapters. These girls?

They’re my whole damn book.

Back then, I walked in worn-out sandals and borrowed confidence. But with them, I stood taller than I ever had. Maybe that’s when I first slipped into my invisible high heels — not of ambition or success yet, but of strength. Of belonging.

We weren’t perfect. We were beautifully messed up — five girls with nothing flawless, but everything priceless. When life threw us deadlines, heartbreaks, and society’s pressure, we survived with one weapon: our gang. Our chai. Our unstoppable, unforgettable sisterhood.

We didn’t just pass exams. We passed life. Together.

Because we weren’t just classmates. We were stories in each other’s diaries — a full syllabus of friendship, drama, samosas, and shared dreams. And that was our real degree.

Still Us

We weren't just friends —

We were lifeboats,

Umbrellas in the wrong seasons,

Maps that led only to each other.

You were my glorious disaster —

And my favourite safe place to land.

Time will play its tricks,

But somewhere, there will always be

That laugh,

That street, that room,

That photograph,

Where we are

Still us.

Chapter - 10

Between Applause and Ambition

After college, life scattered like old project papers — once important, now collecting dust. The laughter that once filled college corridors now felt distant. The five of us who were once inseparable were suddenly busy untangling our own destinies. There were no goodbyes, just missed calls and half-hearted replies. Somewhere between job hunts and final semester blues, misunderstandings crept in. A silence settled, heavy and unfamiliar, where once there had been endless noise.

I heard from a classmate that the four of them were gossiping about me. Maybe it wasn't true. Maybe it was. But it was enough to make me pull away. The silence between us grew longer than our group chats ever did. It felt like a vital part of me had simply vanished, leaving an ache.

I missed them. Terribly. But the thought of backbiting and betrayal was enough to clench my fists in anger. This anger was a shield, protecting the raw wound of absence.

Then came my first job — and with it, a quiet sense of pride. I had bagged the highest salary among all of us. I didn't flaunt it, but a small voice inside whispered, "See? I made it." It was a victory, but a solitary one. No one from the gang is to cheer or spill chai on the celebration.

First Desk, First Dream

The day I received my appointment letter, I read it three times just to see my name printed on official paper. Not handwritten. Not scribbled on a college project. Typed. Signed. Real. That paper wasn't just a letter. It was a promise. A gateway. A tiny piece of proof that my life was moving forward.

On my first day, I walked into the office with nervous lipstick and borrowed confidence. My palms were sweating, my heart was racing, but I wore the calm of a news anchor — trained to smile even when the script is chaos.

My desk was near the window. I had my own desktop. A chair that spun. A drawer that locked. I touched each one like a child discovering new toys. This wasn't just a job. It was my first step toward the life I had imagined — or at least, the life I thought I had imagined. And for a moment, the quiet hum of the office replaced the distant echoes of college laughter, a new kind of silence.

Because in all those dreams, I'd never pictured my boss playing DJ with his own voice or calling me "young blood" while handing me stapler refills. But hey — dreams adjust. And so did I.

From College Corridors to Office Cubicles

They say college is the best time of your life. I didn't fully believe that — until I joined the office and realised I'd traded chai gossip and bunked lectures for Outlook logins and squeaky chairs. The easy camaraderie, the shared eye-rolls over a bad lecture—those were replaced by polite smiles and whispered complaints.

In college, even the worst days had backup plans — a quick samosa, a last-bench nap, or a friend ready to curse the world with you. But in the office? Even the best days came with 17 "quick calls" and a to-do list that regenerated like a Marvel villain. There was no one to nudge under the table, no one to share a silent giggle with when the boss droned on. That kind of shared misery was a comfort I deeply missed.

I had always dreamed of the "best job." You know — blazers, shiny glass cabins, a cool boss who says things like "Take a break, your mental health matters." But instead, I got… him.

My boss. A man who had clearly been my enemy in a past life — back to take revenge, this time using passive-aggressive emails.

He had two permanent moods:

- Bad mood: Grumpy and rude.
- Good mood: Boring and still rude — but now with flashback photos.

"Look at this picture! I was quite the heartthrob in college!" I'd look at the blurry photo of a man with over-gelled hair and a weird pout, trying my best to smile and say, "Wow, sir!" But inside my head? "That's a monkey in a cool shirt with extra buttons open."

I used to giggle silently like a school kid hiding a comic book in class. It was a small act of rebellion, a whisper of my old self in this new, rigid world.

He wasn't completely evil — just painfully self-obsessed and allergic to peace. He'd randomly walk over and say things like: "When I was your age, I managed four departments and still had time to go to the gym." Meanwhile, I was just trying to manage one Excel sheet without crying.

But I didn't quit. Because every time I saw my ID card—my name printed, not scribbled — I remembered how far I'd come.

Unexpected Friendships

But what I didn't have was someone to share it with. I had always been someone who loved to share — good news, bad days, funny chai moments. But after our group drifted apart and small misunderstandings took root, the constant noise of friendship had faded, and a space inside me felt empty, colder than I'd realised.

I tried calling them — one by one — trying to fill that silence. And slowly, I accepted that not everything broken can be repaired… but some cracks let light back in. And this light came from the most unexpected places.

One day, at a common friend's birthday party, I met someone unexpected: my old enemy. We hadn't spoken in four years. Our last memory together had been a heated fight. But that day, we laughed. We laughed over old stories, old versions of ourselves. And slowly — without planning it — we became good friends. It wasn't the boisterous, chaotic laughter of my college gang, but it was real, a gentle balm for a lonely heart.

At the time, I didn't understand why that friendship returned. But now I know: life was preparing me. Sometimes, when storms are coming, life sends umbrellas ahead of time. People. These new connections weren't meant to replace what was lost, but to show me that new forms of support could emerge, filling different kinds of spaces.

In my journey, I've learned that everyone who enters your life has a reason:

- My school principal — who held me up with empathy and helped me finish my studies.
- My Aama — who took responsibility for everything when we were falling apart.
- Srija Chechi — who celebrated every small victory and held my hand in the dark.
- My girl gang — my chaos, my healers, who brought back laughter and madness.

And then — out of the blue — he came into my life again. Sandy. In our group, he was the Richie Rich — deep pockets, deep dimples, and the one who always picked up the bill. Picnic plans? He drove. Movie nights? He paid. Laughter? Always louder when he was around.

But this time, when we reconnected, there was no loud music or pizza boxes. Just two people, quieter than before. He had lost his mother. I had lost mine. We were both empty in different ways — trying hard to live again. It wasn't about romantic drama. It was never that. It was about pure, unsaid understanding. The kind where you just show up — no grand gestures, no expectations — just a quiet promise to be there, even for the smallest need. In our shared silence, a new kind of healing began to bloom, different from the loud, chaotic comfort I once knew.

We spoke less, but felt more. When I broke down, he didn't try to fix me — he just sat beside me. When he needed silence, I gave it without asking why. Maybe that's what healing looks like — two hearts, both bruised, walking beside each other with no map and no questions. Just presence. Together, we started to laugh again. Not like before, but like we were learning how. A quieter, softer laughter, but a genuine one, showing that joy could still find its way back.

"Where Joy Once Lived"

The laughter faded, the echo long,

A silent ache, where joy belonged.

Old paths diverged, a friendship's end,

A lonely journey, without a friend.

Then whispers came, in quiet ways,

New comfort found in unexpected days.

A helping hand, a knowing glance,

A second chance, a gentle dance.

Not loud and bright, like summers past,

But steady light, designed to last.

For even in the deepest night,

New stars can bloom, with tender light.

Chapter - 11

A Story I Didn't Write

"Life doesn't always follow your script. Sometimes, it hands you a surprise scene — and expects you to improvise."

-Muna

It all began at a cousin's wedding. I went for the dance, the dahi vada, and the escape from everyday life. But without realising it, I walked straight into the spotlight.

Somehow, I became the hot topic of the wedding.

Relatives I barely recognised suddenly knew my full name, my marks, my manners, even my favourite colour (which, for the record, no one had asked). "That's Muna," they said proudly, as if I had just returned with a gold medal. "So graceful. Sharp-minded. And have you seen her skin? Shines like *haldi* without even applying it!" My beauty was being described in every household like the newest festive recipe — passed around, exaggerated, and decorated with a little extra *masala*.

I smiled politely. Touched feet. Nodded when they asked if I cooked well. Ate two extra *rasgullas* to stay sane.

But that wasn't the end.

Some called me "perfect." Others said my time had come. The wedding lights hadn't even come down when the proposals started raining. Proposal after proposal. Like chai during college group studies. Like free advice from elders who think marriage is life's biggest achievement. Like overenthusiastic guests who won't leave even after the last *laddoo* is packed.

I was tired of saying no.

And then came The One — the one Baba liked.

"They're a good family," Uncle said to Baba, and his eyes were soft with hope. "Own house, own gym, own car… Your princess will be queen." Some called it a golden opportunity. Others called it fate.

I just called it… annoying.

I wanted to scream: "No! I have dreams! I want to finish my MBA! I'm not ready!"

But Baba looked at me the way only a father can — full of love, pride, and just a little helplessness. His eyes were tired, yet shining — a reflection of years of quiet sacrifice and one soft hope: That maybe, just maybe, one of his daughters could finally rest without worry.

It wasn't pressure. It was longing.

It was trust — that I would make the right choice, not just for me, but for all of us.

"Just meet them once," he said gently. "If something feels wrong, say no. But give them a chance."

I sighed. "Fine. Let them come. I'll say no and close the chapter."

Enter: Nepali Salman Khan

The day arrived like a scene from a low-budget family drama —

Anxious uncles. Overdressed aunties. A table full of dry fruits. And that lingering scent of rosewater mixed with expectation.

They came in a polite procession — shiny shoes, *mithai* boxes wrapped in gold foil, and expressions that had clearly been practised.

I stood at the doorway, pretending to fix my *dupatta*, heart racing like I was about to take an exam I hadn't studied for. I had promised myself I'd act shy and demure — like in those old-school Hindi movies.

And I tried. I did.

But the moment I stepped into the room, the vibe was too much. Everyone sat stiff like a wedding card photo. Their smiles froze. Their eyes are scanning. I couldn't help it — my lips curled, not into the shy smile I'd rehearsed, but into a "What the hell am I doing?" grin.

And then… Nikesh entered.

He wasn't tall — maybe just above my shoulder — but he walked in like height had nothing to do with confidence. Fair, gym-fit, wearing a tight shirt stitched by a tailor who only takes biceps seriously.

And sunglasses. Big, reflective, hero-type sunglasses.

He sat down with folded arms, calm and collected — even the cushions looked nervous.

Then came The Moment.

He slowly removed the sunglasses.

And my brain screamed, “Nepali Salman Khan!”

Because once the shades were off, I saw the real him. Not the “hero” version — the human one.

His eyes — typical Nepali eyes. Small. Soft. Slightly puffy under the lids, like he hadn’t slept… or had cried in secret. The macho mask slipped. What remained was… a boy trying not to try too hard. It was oddly sweet. And it made me relax.

I handed him the tea tray, avoiding eye contact. “I didn’t get off work today,” I mumbled. “So, I’ll leave soon.”

He nodded. No cheesy line. No creepy smile.

Just… silence.

That awkward, respectful silence that said: I’m here because they told me to be here, too.

“Can I drop you off at your office?” he asked, voice gentle.

I didn’t look up, but something about him felt… calm. In a room full of noise, he was the still note. And strangely, the one that lingered.

And I?

I sat there — one foot in the dream I’d had since Class 8B, and the other tangled in a room full of rose petals and pressure.

The truth?

It's not that I didn't want love. Or a partner.

A small part of me even liked the drama — The way everyone smiled when I entered. The way they whispered about my beauty. The way Baba looked was proud—like he'd painted the perfect future on the canvas of that moment.

But beneath the sweetness, there was a quiet fear: I didn't want to be trapped in a story that wasn't mine.

After that, I gave my answer. "I'm not ready. I want to complete my MBA. I haven't even started my life yet." A deep breath, a quiet word – and a wave of relief washed over me. It felt like I'd just stepped out from under a heavy, unseen weight.

Royal Lunch, Raw Doubts

Two months passed. No contact from Nikesh's family. I thought it was over. But silence, it turns out, was just the interval — not the end.

Suddenly, an invite arrived: Lunch at Nikesh's house.

I smelled something fishy. But Aama and Baba said, "We can't say no. Parents of three daughters don't show attitude."

So, we went.

The house looked like a set — half soap opera, half silent test. Too many cushions. Too many smiles. Too many expectations folded into crisp sarees and polished tea trays.

Their house was elegant — one of those places where even the curtains behave. Everything matched. Even the spoons sparkled.

A home that whispered: “Behave. You’re being watched.”

I wore a red and beige salwar suit — formal enough to say I cared, casual enough to say I had options.

Then I smelled the *pulao*.

Not ordinary *pulao*. Dry fruits. Saffron. Ghee.

Royalty on a plate.

And that was just the trailer. There were four types of sabzi, paneer melting in orange cream, puris puffed to perfection, and a dessert table that could cater for a small wedding.

And the cherry on top?

The maid had been working since morning. Till 5 PM. For one lunch.

I wanted to cry. Not from emotion — from hope. Maybe marriage doesn’t mean kitchen duty after all.

I scanned the room like a detective on mute.

Nikesh’s mother was warm but strategic — the kind who compliments your outfit and then asks how well you make *rotis*.

His sister was cheerful — already smiling like we’d share lipstick secrets.

Nikesh… no hero entry this time.

Just a simple *kurta*. And a look that said: *Let's survive this.*

Then came the part I dreaded: "Let them talk in private."

I protested, "No, I'm fine here."

But the pressure was soft and sticky — like *rasgulla.*

Too sweet to refuse. Too much to escape.

We were led to a quiet sitting room with polished furniture and an air freshener that smelled like polite pressure.

I sat down and immediately started peeling off my nail polish — chipped, like my mental state.

Nikesh spoke first:

"If you want to study more, I'll support that. Everyone already likes you."

I didn't respond. Just kept working on that stubborn thumbnail.

He noticed.

A minute later, he returned with a bottle of pink nail polish.

"My sister's," he said, handing it to me. "You can reapply."

We both laughed — really laughed.

Not a romantic moment. But a real one.

It didn't fix everything. But it softened something.

I looked at him and said honestly, “I need at least two more years. I have plans.”

He nodded. “Okay.”

We walked back out. And the drama started.

“She needs time,” he told everyone. “She can study after marriage, too.”

Suddenly, the house turned into a motivational rally.

Tears. Applause. Speeches. “Don’t let this go!” “He’s a gem!” “You’ll never get a better house than this!” “Your father has three daughters!” “They’re giving you freedom. What more do you want?” “Such chances don’t come twice…”

After being emotionally bowled for two hours, I whispered, “Okay…”

The room erupted.

Sweets. *Dupattas* flying. One aunt cried.

And Baba? He smiled like a mountain had been lifted from his chest.

But me?

I stood in the middle.

Smiling.

Still unsure.

Still peeling something invisible off my heart.

Had I just stepped into a beautiful life…

Or quietly stepped out of my own?

A Quiet Question

A few days later, we had a small ceremony — like a *roka.*

I was the centre of attention.

Compliments came from every corner. "She's glowing," someone said. "Such a lucky girl," another whispered.

And I smiled. I posed. I played the part.

That night, sitting alone — makeup half on, bangles still clinking — a quiet question crawled into my chest:

Am I rushing too fast?

Nikesh seemed kind. His family was warm. He had his own business. He said I could study. There was even a maid who stayed till 5 p.m. Everything looked like a perfect.

So why did I feel like I was holding my breath?

I shared the news with my girl gang — expecting squeals, hugs. Pavi asked softly, "Don't you think you're rushing? You're just 20." I took it the wrong way — thought they were laughing at me again.

Jo said, "If you're happy, then okay. It's your life."

I nodded. But deep inside, I asked myself — *Am I really happy?*

I didn't know. I started convincing myself: He's supportive. His family's kind. I can study after marriage…

But something still didn't sit right. The fairy tale felt too rehearsed. And I wasn't sure… Who wrote my lines?

A Path Unchosen

A golden cage, it looks so bright,

A borrowed joy, a painted light.

Cheers ring loud, a happy noise,

But quiet worries fill my joys.

A future planned seems good and clear,

But inner whispers ask, Whose life is here?

My own true heart, a wide, vast space,

Can this new story find its place?

Chapter - 12

Gift-Wrapped Dreams

Sometimes, the choices that shape your life don't feel like choices at all.

They arrive quietly — wrapped in love, sealed with tradition, and handed over like a gift you're expected to cherish. You smile. You nod. And somewhere between gratitude and guilt, your voice gets folded away.

Some fairy tales don't end with glass slippers. Some begin when you realise your shoes no longer fit.

When It First Felt Real

After the emotional rally and my quiet "Okay…" to the proposal, a new chapter began. Not loud or dramatic — just slow and soft.

For a moment, I wondered if I'd made the biggest mistake of my life… or if this quiet surrender was actually the bravest thing I'd ever done.

Then, like a gentle current, Nikesh's messages started coming in — carrying a cautious kind of hope I didn't know I needed.

It began with late-night calls, simple conversations.

He wasn't poetic, but he was present. Like a quiet melody humming in the background.

He even came to meet me — not for a grand gesture, just an easy, official date. We went to a movie. He introduced me to his friends and said, "This is your sister-in-law." There were no big words, no overacting. Just a calm, simple connection. We talked about work, movies, and what we'd eat if calories didn't exist. Where we might travel one day.

One night, he called out of the blue.

"Who's your favourite hero?"

"John Abraham," I said.

"And if you had to choose between him and me?"

I laughed. "John, obviously."

He pretended to sulk. "Well, if it were me choosing… I'd still pick you."

It was silly. Soft. But something about it settled in my heart. Maybe… this could be something real. I laughed a little more. Worried a little less. Slowly, I was swept into the whirlwind of love. .

I used to dismiss those who said they felt butterflies. To me, it sounded so dramatic—a mere Bollywood fantasy. But then, I understood. They fluttered every time he whispered my name, that gentle tone like he was still discovering what it truly meant—to him, to us.

I didn't know the rulebook. How much to show? What was too eager, what was not enough. But I gave what I had — hoping it would be enough. Even love songs I used to skip… now felt like they were written for us. And slowly, my wild, colourful dreams — the bold ones—started getting folded away. My dream of working in an ad agency, creating campaigns, wearing crisp formals, flying off to meetings —

It wasn't thrown out. It was folded. Neatly. Reverently.

Each crease was a small goodbye to a version of me I had once believed I could still be. They became like old letters — precious, heavy — kept in a drawer you don't open often.

Because for now… I was Cinderella.

And this was the ball.

And Then, Reality Knocked

One afternoon, I was told they'd be calling to ask what kind of saree I wanted for the wedding. I smiled. Imagined soft pastels or deep, dark pink silk. Maybe something light with a gold border. I even looked up blouse designs online.

But instead of a call… I got a bag.

The saree, jewellery, shoes — everything had already been bought. I held it — a beautiful, heavy bag. The silk felt stiff in my hands, the smell of new zari strong in the air. It wasn't just fabric. It was a decision, wrapped and ready, that I hadn't even been part of.

I smiled. I said thank you. I nodded, like a good girl.

But inside me — something didn't just crack.

It splintered.

This was every girl's day. The one she has dreamed of since childhood. And yet… I wasn't even asked what colour I wanted to remember it in. I had imagined choosing the earrings I'd wear when Baba looked at me with tears. The lipstick that would survive Aama's hug. The saree I'd wrap around years later and whisper, *"This was mine."*

But none of it was mine. Not a thread. Not a shimmer. Not a single sparkle that whispered my name.

Maybe they loved me.

Maybe they believed they were giving me the best.

But no one asked what perfect looked like to me. There were so many things that didn't feel right. They said my family would cover all wedding expenses. But why? We were both getting married — shouldn't it be shared?

I asked if we could reduce the guest list.

They said, "How can we disappoint our guests?"

Baba managed everything, silently, like he always did. But the silence I swallowed that day… tasted like a goodbye I hadn't rehearsed.

That's when I understood —

It's not the absence of gold that hurts. It's the absence of your voice while someone else decides how you should shine.

The Wedding Day: The Red Saree

I stood in front of the mirror — draped in red, glitter in my eyes, and a quiet ache blooming in my chest.

I looked complete.

But I didn't feel whole.

My smile held, but I wasn't sure if it was real or just well-practised.

My dreams had been folded into this moment. One pleat at a time.

Pima and Yashu — my sisters — cried loudly. It didn't feel like a celebration. It felt like mourning. Their tears weren't just for the bride in red. They were for every bedtime secret, every shared laugh, every little fight. I had always been the thread holding us together. And now, they were unravelling.

Aama had been crying for days — not in front of me, but in small ways. In how she touched my hand while cutting vegetables. In the way she avoided looking at my packed suitcase. She wasn't just losing a daughter. She was losing her gossip partner, her second pair of hands.

My girl gang arrived. Their hugs were longer. Their eyes, louder. When I hugged them, something inside me cracked — Like someone had pressed rewind on all our late nights, inside jokes, broken hearts, and shared Maggi. And deep inside that hug was something I didn't expect: Regret. For the distance I had let grow. For not listening when they were always right.

Sandy tried to lighten the mood.

"You don't even look like a bride — this feels like child marriage," he said.

"At least now, I'll have one less headache."

We laughed. That bittersweet kind of laugh. Because maybe I was still a child. Just dressed better. I wasn't just leaving them. I was leaving behind pieces of me I didn't know how to carry forward.

Vishnu and Sujan — my brothers — were dancing, joking, pretending nothing big was happening.

But Baba…

He didn't cry. He managed everything. The guests. The food. The chaos. Holding his pain like a wall — solid, unshaken. As if emotions could wait until logistics were done. When it was time, he gently pushed me into the car. I hugged him tight, hoping he'd crack. But he didn't. And that's when I whispered my first goodbye. The kind where nothing feels good. Nikesh was smiling. He promised to take care of me.

Maybe he meant it.

Maybe, for now, that was enough.

But as the car pulled away, I looked back — one last time.

At my house. At my people. At every version of me I was leaving behind.

And I wondered:

What was I leaving behind?

And who was I becoming?

The answer felt like a breath held.

A story unwritten.

Waiting for the next page. The car pulled away. My smile stayed. But inside, I wasn't sure if I was a bride, a child, or a stranger wearing red.

The Saree I Didn't Choose

They dressed me in red, in stories and silk,
But no one asked how I dreamed I'd look.
They said, "You shine," and I smiled back,
While stitching my silence into the pleats, I wore.

I waved goodbye with painted hands,
To sisters who cried like I never would.
To friends whose laughter I left behind,
And a mother who mourned her friend in silence.

I was the queen in someone else's script,
Wearing jewels I didn't choose.
And as the music faded and the car pulled away —
I wondered if I was walking toward love…
Or away from the girl I used to be.

Chapter - 13

When the Fairy Tale Cracked

"Some days, you don't say goodbye to people.

You say goodbye to the person you were with."

Sometimes, the scariest part of a fairy tale isn't the villain—it's the shattering silence after the story ends, when the applause dies, no one looks back... and you're left alone with a smile that cuts. Or maybe, the scariest part is when you realise the fairy tale itself was never truly yours, but a script handed to you, with your role already decided.

The New Home

After two and a half hours, the car finally stopped, depositing me at my new home in Devlali Camp, Nashik. The house pulsed with excited relatives, a sea of unfamiliar faces and expectant smiles. Rituals blurred into a kaleidoscope of colours and scents; sweets were pressed into my hands, and laughter echoed, bright and insistent, down the halls. But beneath the surface, a colder truth settled: my surname had changed. My mailing address. My very family. The place I'd known for two decades was now... a distant memory.

The first few days spun by like a dream. I was the new bride—centre of attention, pampered, showered with compliments. Nikesh was warm, attentive, his presence a comforting anchor in this dizzying shift. But then, as subtly as dust motes in sunlight, the music began to fade. Reality didn't knock; it began to creep in, first through the kitchen doors.

The Erosion of Self

I had been fiercely independent since sixteen. I'd earned my own money, managed my life, carved my path. But here, suddenly, I was... jobless. It wasn't just that I had nothing; it was that I felt like I was nothing. No salary, no name on an office ID, no schedule to follow. Instead, I inherited a long list of unwritten rules—each one a silent instruction on who I could no longer be.

Everyone became my personal trainer, correcting my methods, commenting on my every move. It was as if my entire twenty years before marriage had been one long, fundamental mistake. I tried harder, worked longer, cooked better—but it was never enough. Slowly, almost imperceptibly, I began to lose my spark. Then, my confidence. My laughter faded, replaced by a hollow silence. My shoulders curled inward, my eyes avoided mirrors. I was forgetting the girl I used to be—the one who stood tall, who believed she could be anything. Even holding a pen, once an extension of my ambition, felt heavy, alien, like it no longer belonged in my hand.

The Illusion Shatters

Finally, I took a desperate step. I told Nikesh I wanted to study further.

“I know,” he said. “Let’s start.”

That one sentence, simple as it was, gave me a gasp of breath again. I enrolled in entrance classes.

On the first day, my mother-in-law smiled, “Wow, you took admission. Very good. Study well.” Then, casually: “But before you go, hope you’ll prepare breakfast.”

I forced a smile. Why only me? My sister-in-law often woke at ten or even eleven-thirty. No one asked her to lift a spoon. But me? At seven a.m., I was in the kitchen. Did they not eat before I arrived? Or were they all waiting for the bahu to cook?

One afternoon, after cooking, I politely asked, "Would you like lunch now? I'm about to start studying; just let me know if you need anything."

"No, no. You go study," she waved me off.

Ten minutes later, my name was shouted. “Yes?”

"I'm hungry. Serve lunch."

I served, asked, "Do you need anything else?"

“No,” she said. Five minutes later: “Give me roti.” Then: “Water.” Then: “Remote.”

Every trivial demand chipped away at me. My dreams felt impossibly far. My books remained untouched. And my fairy tale? It was twisting into a horror story.

I’d wake before dawn, cook breakfast for everyone, then rush to class without a single bite. I missed home with an ache that deepened each day. Baba hadn't cried at the wedding, but after all the relatives left, I heard him—weeping quietly over the small, ordinary things.

Even when everyone else was judging, my father-in-law treated me with quiet kindness—not like the others. He never interfered, never questioned, but his care felt like a small, steady refuge in the chaos.

I bottled it all up, the silent screams, the mounting despair—until one day, our maid, bless her simple honesty, casually asked, "Why do you make so much breakfast every day? They usually bring it from outside. And the one you make… they just pack it up and give it to me."

I froze. "What?"

She shrugged. "Yes, madam. Most days."

Every day, my mother-in-law had given me different, elaborate breakfast requests—as if I was cooking for a restaurant. The truth hit me: she didn't want me to succeed. It wasn't about cooking or chores; it was about control.

The Ultimate Demand

Then came the PCOD. Every month, my periods would miss, and every month, their hopes, unspoken but palpable, grew higher. When I finally gathered the courage to tell my mother-in-law about my condition, she screamed:

"Why didn't you tell us before marriage? You've ruined my son's life! If you don't give me a baby in two years, I'll make him remarry."

I broke. Shattered. I cried, a raw, uncontrollable sob, and said I was sorry, even though I had no idea what I was apologising for. My mental health, already fragile, began to slip through the cracks. Every day became a battlefield—a relentless assault of pain, physical, emotional, and invisible to everyone else.

Nikesh tried to comfort me; his voice a balm that couldn't reach the wound.

"Don't worry, Mumma is just a little loud. We'll start medication. Once she has a grandson, she'll calm down."

And through it all, not once did anyone ask—Muna, what do you want?

Everyone outside thought I was living a perfect life—big house, loving husband, a dream come true. But inside, I was shrinking, day by day, into nothing. Nikesh had started ignoring me. His silence became another suffocating weight on my chest.

And my mother-in-law never missed a chance to deliver her final, crushing blow:

"You behave like this because you don't have a mother to teach you."

Every time she said it, my heart didn't just ache; it screamed, a silent, furious wail: *But you have your mother. Why didn't she teach you kindness? Empathy? Respect?—or even how to treat your daughter-in-law?*"

Trapped in their fairy tale script, I might not rewrite the whole story today, but I was absolutely done playing someone I wasn't.

The Bride Who Forgot to Breathe

I wore the red, but not the smile.

They saw the shimmer, not the trial.

I served with hands that longed to write,

I cooked their peace and swallowed the fight.

They dressed me up, called me their pride—

While slowly, I died from the inside.

Not once did they ask what lived in me,

A girl, a dream, a wish to be free.

But from the cracks, where I was thrown,

A voice still whispered—I am my own.

Chapter - 14

A Whisper in the Womb

"Hope is the thing with feathers that perches in the soul—and sings the tune without the words—and never stops at all."

— Emily Dickinson

After three years of chasing faint lines on pregnancy kits—always blank, always negative—I had stopped counting.

I'd changed doctors like seasons, swallowed powders that tasted like regret, and clung to pills that promised miracles. I lay on clinic beds under flickering tube lights, with cold gel on my stomach and colder silence inside me. Each scan ended the same — just me, my tears, and another cruel "No."

Every "No" whispered louder:

"You are not enough."

I wasn't just exhausted by tests or medicines. I was tired of living as if my worth depended on two pink lines.

My mother-in-law's taunts started before sunrise:

"Give me a grandson first. Then live your life."

Sweet on the surface, sharp underneath — her words were sugar-coated blades.

The dining table felt quieter. The bed felt colder. And the weight of waiting was heavier than my own body.

Then came the doctor's final suggestion — laparoscopy.

"It's a minor surgery," he said.

Hope didn't answer. Despair did.

I agreed without hesitation. My body had ceased to be my own long ago.

The surgery came and went. Still, nothing changed.

Until one dizzy morning, when I felt... different. I assumed it was exhaustion, or maybe another day of crying myself sick.

But the feeling stayed.

Out of weary habit, not hope, I dragged myself to the doctor again.

When he returned with my results, his smile said it before his words did.

"Congratulations. You're pregnant."

I blinked.

"What?"

He nodded. "Yes. I'm sure."

I made him double-check.

Then triple-check.

After years of "No," even a "Yes" felt unfamiliar.

I walked out in a daze — wanting to laugh, cry, fall to my knees, or scream thank you to the sky. I felt a profound relief, thanking God multiple times for answering my prayers. That night, for the first time in years, I rested my hand on my belly not in pain, but in prayer. For the first time, I didn't feel broken. I felt... chosen.

The news rippled through the house like a sudden burst of sunshine. My mother-in-law, who had been a storm cloud for years, actually embraced me, her voice softening as she murmured blessings. My father-in-law clapped Nikesh on the back, and even the usual silence of the dining table was replaced by an uncharacteristic buzz of shared excitement. For a fleeting moment, I felt not just chosen, but truly welcomed into their fold, as if this tiny life inside me had finally paved the way for acceptance.

But joy, I've learned, isn't a full stop.

It's a pause — brief and often interrupted. This fleeting warmth lasted only a few days.

In my in-laws' eyes, my pregnancy wasn't joy. It was justification.

"Now behave." "No more drama." "You got what you wanted."

For a few days, they treated me like fragile glass. By the second week, their sharp words returned, dressed in new phrases. Pregnancy didn't end the cruelty. It simply gave it a new context.

Still, I found one ritual that saved me —

Late at night, when the house slept and my heart stayed wide awake, I spoke to the tiny life inside me:

"Hi, baby. It's just us. But I promise — you're already loved."

That was my safest moment of the day.

Nikesh, though, had begun to change.

I still remember how excited he was the day we got the news. The doctor had recommended eating more fruits, and after dropping me home, he rushed to the market like a man on a mission. Apples, watermelons, sweet limes, strawberries, plums, bananas, oranges — he bought everything he could find. Our dining table turned into a fruit cart overnight. He was into fitness, so he made two bowls — one for him, one for me — and we sat quietly eating like we had crossed into a new chapter.

In that moment, I thought maybe everything would finally be fine. Maybe my in-laws would accept me now. That maybe... this baby would make everything right.

But that hope was short-lived. He was quiet. But now his silence carried weight. Distance. Mood swings. Cold replies.

I had dreamt of shared hospital visits, cravings met with late-night ice cream runs, foot rubs, and silly baby fights. But all I had were solo rickshaw rides and unanswered messages.

Was it the hormones, or simply heartbreak layered over years finally surfacing?

I couldn’t eat. My childhood hyperacidity came back with a force. I threw up whatever I forced down. My body ached, my soul screamed, but my surroundings stayed indifferent.

I once believed pregnancy would heal everything. But now I knew — nothing grows in poisoned soil.

To make it worse, everyone suddenly became an expert on my womb.

"Don’t eat mangoes." "Tamarind will harm the baby." "Too much sugar? You’ll regret it." "Don’t rest so much, you’ll end up needing surgery."

Even when the doctor advised four months of bed rest, my mother-in-law scoffed:

"Doctors just want money. I worked through all three of my pregnancies. Get up. Move."

Her pride stories stabbed deeper than my fatigue ever could.

I tried to explain, my voice thin with exhaustion, "Doctor said, I need rest."

But my truth was too inconvenient for their comfort.

My body was shutting down.

But my spirit? That was already numb.

Every night, I whispered to the one who truly heard me—my baby.

And in those moments, I felt alive.

As a first-time mother, every emotion was new.

I had no guidebook. No hand to hold.

And the one who should've stood beside me — had drifted far.

Nikesh wasn't just distracted. He was... changing.

Arguments began over nothing.

Caring words vanished.

His presence felt like an absence.

It scared me — not just what was happening between us, but what it hinted at. Still, I had to choose.

I could waste energy decoding his behaviour...Or I could protect the life quietly blooming inside me. And so, I spoke to my baby. I didn't always get answers. But I always felt heard.

"In the quiet of those nights, a mother was truly born."

Poem: I Found My Home

They called it a blessing,

But treated me like a burden.

They smiled for the world,

but sighed behind my back.

I wanted care,

I got commands.

I wanted peace,

I got prescriptions from people wearing love like a costume.

But when the world went quiet,

And it was just you and me in the stillness,

I found my home —

not in these walls,

But in the rhythm of your heartbeat.

You're not just a baby.

You're my rescue.

My reminder.

My reason.

The only one

Who chose me

Without conditions.

Chapter - 15

The Bitter Awakening

"Sometimes, the loudest rebellion is choosing yourself in silence."

It was my third month of pregnancy. One day, my father-in-law left for a business trip. My mother-in-law and sister-in-law had also gone out. The house was unusually quiet. Only three of us remained: me, Nikesh, and his distant cousin, Sweety.

She was 16 or 17, left in my care so I could guide her in her studies, help her become more responsible. Her father believed I could bring her focus back to the right path. She had a reputation for multiple love affairs at such a young age, but I tried not to judge. I wanted to believe she had come into our home to learn.

But she hadn't come to grow.

She had come to unravel.

At first, I tried to guide her gently. I helped her with her books, encouraged her to dream bigger. But she was uninterested in learning—and certainly uninterested in me. Her attention lay elsewhere.

And slowly, I noticed: she was far too comfortable with Nikesh.

Slowly, I began noticing her comfort with Nikesh. Too comfortable.

One afternoon, I walked in with his lunch. The casual intimacy of the scene stopped me cold in the doorway. She was on the floor beside him, almost leaning against his knee, her laughter light and unburdened. Her fingers, so familiar in their gesture, brushed something from his shoulder, a touch that lingered, possessive. He didn't flinch. He didn't even look guilty. A strange, bitter taste filled my mouth, and the plate in my hand felt suddenly heavy, precarious. I told myself they were cousins, that this was just their way, a cultural closeness I was misinterpreting. It’s the hormones, I whispered to myself, the pregnancy making me paranoid. I tried to push the image away, to believe in the innocence I desperately craved.

But then one day, while on a call, my gaze drifted towards the living room. My breath hitched. There it was: a quick, almost imperceptible gesture from her, a playful flick of her wrist, and then, his answering, unmistakable flying kiss. My heart didn't just pound; it slammed against my ribs, a frantic drumbeat of disbelief. The air seemed to thicken, suddenly too heavy to breathe. My hands clenched, the phone almost slipping from my grasp. I blinked, again and again, willing the image to disappear, to be a trick of light, a figment of my overwrought mind. But once doubt settles, it doesn't leave quietly. I started observing more.

They went out together. Came back together. They teased each other. Laughed like teenagers. And when he was with me, he was distant, glued to his phone. Once, we had known each other's passwords, shared every whispered dream in the dark. Now, everything was hidden. My husband was becoming a stranger.

Slowly, insidiously, Sweety began to take over my small, intimate roles—the ones that had felt like threads weaving me into the fabric of our life together. She started making his morning protein shake, a ritual I'd always cherished, the quiet hum of the blender a familiar start to our day. Now, her laughter would drift from the kitchen as she prepared it. Then came his favourite sabzi, the one I'd spent hours perfecting just for his taste. I'd watch them at the table, a phantom ache in my hands, feeling the bitter taste of my own irrelevance. And the evening head massage, our quiet, unspoken communion, became hers too. Each stolen act felt like a tiny, deliberate cut, severing a piece of me from him, from us. With each passing day, I felt less like his wife, less like myself, and more like a silent, unseen guest in my own marriage, watching my life unfold without me.

I had just begun smiling again after so much pain. But watching them hurt in ways I couldn't put into words. It was like being stabbed slowly, every day. My heart raced. My body trembled. I felt like I was standing near a fire, unable to move away.

One night, I gathered the courage to talk to Nikesh. I stood outside the kitchen, rehearsing my words like a script. But what do you say when your suspicion wears your husband's perfume?

He was drinking water when I spoke. In a flash, he hurled the glass against the wall. It shattered. Like me.

"Your dirty mind can only think dirty things!" he screamed.

The glass shattered, echoing in the sudden, dreadful silence. The crash filled the silence. Broken pieces lay on the floor — just like my hope.. His furious breathing filled the void. I stood there, utterly paralysed, the sting of his words sharper than any physical blow. My throat felt thick, raw, as if I'd swallowed glass. I wanted to scream, to cry, to run, but my body wouldn't obey. All I could do was stand, a silent casualty of his rage and my own crumbling world. My mind raced, searching for any crack in the wall of my suspicion, any reason to believe his fury was righteous, not a shield.

He's stressed. I'm overthinking. . He loves me. This is just a misunderstanding.

I repeated these phrases like a mantra, a desperate prayer against the rising tide of dread. I wanted to believe him so fiercely that I forced myself to. I ignored every proof that had been accumulating, every quiet observation. I swallowed every scream that threatened to erupt from my chest. I chose trust – not because I believed him, not because his words held any truth, but because the alternative, the truth itself, was a gaping maw I couldn't bear to look into. It was easier to live in a fragile lie than face the shattering reality.

Days passed. I moved like a ghost through my own home.

Then came a miracle. A reason to breathe again. My son. My Adhyan. My Addhu.

The day he was born, everything else faded. In caring for him, I lost track of everything else. I was a new mother, learning every single fact about this tiny human, navigating the overwhelming exhaustion of late-night cries and the sheer joy of his smallest movements. I didn't have time to think of betrayal, or pain, or even recovery. Every day brought something new. Today, he smiled. Tomorrow, he responded to my voice. The next day, he tried to hold up his neck. I watched him sleep, a tiny smile playing on his lips, and felt a warmth spread through me that nothing else could touch. When he started making happy gurgling sounds, my heart swelled a pure, unadulterated joy. Postpartum was messy. Medicines made me dizzy. But my Addhu gave me something no one else had:

A reason to start again. A reason to survive. A reason to feel whole. Even when everything else was broken.

Baba held him and said, "It feels like I'm holding my Muna again." He looked like me. His nose, his eyes, his tiny face.

There were days I couldn't tell if I was healing or just surviving.

Like most Indian families, it was decided that I would go to my maternal home for my delivery. Baba was waiting. And with him — my siblings, my girl gang, Aama, Srija Chechi, and Sandy. They walked with me, made me laugh, fed every craving, and filled my days with the kind of love I had forgotten existed. I didn't share anything with them. I just believed what I wanted to believe — that Nikesh would never do something like that. Maybe I had misunderstood. That things would go back to normal.

When Addhu arrived, he brought a blinding, overwhelming joy. His eyes, his nose — all mine, a tiny replica of the hope I had almost lost. Nikesh started visiting every weekend, stepping into my maternal home with a practised smile, playing the role of the doting father, the concerned husband. He'd hold Addhu, talk of mundane things, acting as if the gaps between us didn't exist, as if his cousin wasn't still residing in our home, a silent, living monument to my pain. And I, desperately clinging to the illusion of a family, played along. I smiled, I nodded, I pretended to believe his casual affection was real, even as a cold dread whispered that this 'normal' was just a performance, a prolonged goodbye.

Weeks bled into months. Five months. And with each passing visit, the unspoken question grew heavier between us. He never once discussed taking me and Addhu back. When I finally gathered the courage to ask, the words were a hesitant whisper, and he simply ignored me, his gaze sliding away. And the cruellest confirmation: Sweety was still staying at our house. In that moment, the last weak thread of denial snapped. I realised – maybe it was never my imagination. Maybe my silence wasn't protecting anything anymore. It was only suffocating me.

Poem: Shattered, Not Silenced

I saw them laugh in the corners where I once stood.

I watched him change, while I stayed misunderstood.

The glass broke before my heart did, but only just.

And I kept trusting, not because he earned it —

But because I had to survive.

They stole my silence, but they didn't steal my soul.

Because from the ruins came my reason to live.

Tiny fingers, a mirrored smile, a heartbeat that healed me —

not with promises, but with presence.

And though I was shattered, I was never truly gone.

I was just becoming someone unbreakable.

Chapter - 16

Saved by a Voice

"Sometimes, the only way to find light is to become it."

Seven months passed, leaving me emptier than before.

At my maternal home, everything looked fine—on the surface.

Aama once more filled my plate with warm meals. Baba began speaking Addhu's language—a soft babble that melted his usual sternness. My sisters became part-time nannies, washing his tiny clothes with extra care and extra Dettol, rocking him to sleep in turns. Even my brothers—once allergic to emotional display—grinned like little boys every time he babbled or stretched out his arms. Baba's house was filled with joy and laughter.

All because of Addhu.

But beneath that joy, my heart beat with a quiet ache—a sadness no one else could hear.

At night, when the lights dimmed and silence took over, my mind screamed. I'd lie awake, staring at the ceiling, listening to the tick of the clock, to Addhu's soft breathing, and to the ache that no lullaby could hush.

Neighbours had started whispering: "When is your husband coming to take you back?"

Each time, my chest tightened. Their words were like cold drops of rain slipping beneath my skin. I smiled. Nodded. Deflected.

But deep down, I felt like a guest in my own life—uncertain if I was healing or just hiding.

Still, Addhu kept our world turning.

He wasn't even crawling, yet his coos and kicks made the walls feel alive again. His laughter became the answer to every unasked question. My family never made me feel like a burden.

Baba would simply say, "Take care of yourself, chhori. He needs a strong mother."

And then, one day, my father-in-law arrived. He had just returned from a long trip. He didn't say much. He looked at me—really looked. Then he turned to Addhu, a softness spreading across his face.

He sat beside us, held Addhu's tiny hand in his own, and quietly said:

"Come on, it's time to go home."

There was no blame in his tone, no demand. Just a peaceful call.

After months, someone from that house finally saw me—not as a mistake or a burden, but as a human being. A woman who was tired and simply longed for peace.

He hadn't come to take back a daughter-in-law. He came to bring home his daughter—and his grandson.

When we returned to that house, Nikesh had arranged a welcome party: balloons, toys, and a tiny cupboard overflowing with baby clothes. I stood there, Addhu in my arms, and thought maybe God had finally shown me mercy.

But joy, I would learn, is a guest that never stays long.

The cycle returned.

Cooking. Cleaning. Rocking Addhu through endless nights. His dust allergies turned every week into a new battle—medicine, worry, sleep-deprived mornings.

At my maternal home, Aama had been my shield. Here, I was alone.

My mother-in-law loved the idea of a baby—but not the responsibility: not the fevers, not the cries, not the nights that felt like years.

My body—already weary—began to betray me again.

And Nikesh...

He picked fights over everything—why the cupboard was messy, why the food wasn't hot, why I dared to nap during the day.

But I saw it.

He wasn't fighting me.

He was performing—for her. For Sweety.

To show her everything between us was falling apart.

He cursed my parents—the very people who gave me life—as if their love was weakness, their values a joke.

He mocked the way I spoke, the way I sat, the way I existed.

His words were sharp, cold, and loud—louder than my dignity could bear.

And still, I stayed.

At first, I told myself: Maybe it's just anger. Maybe I said something wrong. Maybe if I stay quiet, it'll pass.

But it didn't.

The arguments became insults. The insults became shouting. And then—shouting became silence.

My silence.

Until one day, it wasn't just words anymore.

It was hands.

It was walls.

It was bruised you couldn't see—but I felt every time I moved, every time I breathed.

I stayed quiet—not because I was weak.

But because I kept hoping.

That maybe love could fix what violence had broken. But silence had started to choke me.

I was disappearing—right in front of my child.

And I couldn't vanish.

Not like this.

Not for him.

But whenever I tried to speak, it only made things worse.

My tears, my voice, my truth—turned into weapons used against me.

I wasn't just unheard. I was blamed.

Blamed for feeling. Blamed for seeing. Blamed for existing.

Nikesh had once held my hand, looked into my eyes, and promised me happiness. He'd tattooed my name on his skin—permanent, proud.

As if to say: You're mine forever.

And yet…

Sometimes I'd watch him touch someone else, smile at her, laugh with her…

And I'd look at that tattoo and wonder:

Isn't my name burning his skin?

Isn't it stopping him?

Does ink mean nothing when the heart forgets?

That was the cruellest part.

Not the betrayal. Not the violence.

But that love—once shouted from rooftops—

could vanish so silently,

while my name still stayed on his body.

The Breaking Point

One morning, Nikesh left for the "gym." Sweety, for classes, as usual, went with him. But then the gym trainer knocked.

"Why hasn't Dada been coming lately?"

I froze.

"He left this morning at 7, like always."

The trainer shook his head.

"Always??? He hardly comes anymore."

My world didn't just break—it shattered.

I confessed everything to my in-laws.

My voice trembled with truth.

Nikesh lied. Spun his usual web.

And once again, I was blamed.

For seeing too much.

For speaking too soon.

For daring to break the silence.

Invisible.

Unheard.

Alone.

The bathroom became my only refuge. Inside, I broke down—loud, raw sobs that emptied my chest like a storm collapsing on itself.

In those moments, I wasn't a mother. Or a wife. Or a woman. I was a fading whisper. Held to this world by the thinnest thread.

The Edge

One afternoon, when Addhu, 18 months old, had finally fallen asleep after a long battle of lullabies and back pats, he slept peacefully in my lap. I kissed his forehead, rose to finish chores.

Passing the hallway—I heard it.

Muffled giggles.

Nikesh.

Sweety.

Behind a closed door.

That sound wasn't just laughter. It was a match dropped into a barrel of gunpowder. My heart pounded like a trapped bird. My legs buckled. My skin burned from the inside. Tears slipped quietly down my cheeks, and the world blurred.

I couldn't hear my own thoughts. Couldn't feel the ground.

It brought every unhealed scar back to life.

I stood frozen, the memories crashing down like waves: My mother's death. My shattered dreams. The PCOD. The abuse. The betrayal. The silence.

I whispered to God, "Why me? Again? Haven't I suffered enough? How many times must I wipe my own tears? When will the 'this too shall pass' actually pass?"

Motivational speeches felt like noise. Prayers felt like jokes. Hope felt like cruelty.

That day, I didn't want to survive another round of heartbreak. I didn't want to explain, defend, or pretend. I didn't want to whisper strength into myself one more time. I was exhausted — not just in my body, but in my soul.

I walked to the kitchen. Opened the drawer. Took the sharpest knife.

Held it to my wrist. Just as the cold steel kissed my skin—angry, tired, and done. No trembling.

No tears. Just quietly resolve.

And then… I heard it.

"Mumma! Mumma!"

It was Addhu.

His voice—sharp, clear, full of life—cut through the fog like a blade of light.

The cold steel fell from my hand, clattering to the floor. Not out of fear, but because love screamed louder than silence

My knees gave in, but I didn't fall—I ran.

Not just to him.

Back to myself. Stumbled into the room.

He was sitting upright, his tiny arms outstretched, eyes barely open. His cry wasn't just sound—it was a lifeline. I scooped him into my arms, pressed him to my chest like a prayer.

He wrapped his little fingers around my hair and pressed his face into my neck.

His scent wrapped around me… baby powder, fresh cotton, the milky sweetness only a mother knows. And I felt how life smells.

And just like that, the storm paused.

Not cleared, not ended. But paused.

The Resurrection

He didn't speak. He didn't ask. But in that moment, his little cry echoed louder than all the noise in my head.

Something shifted.

Not all at once. Not like magic. But a thread of light pierced through my cracked self.

He smiled. And in that smile, I didn't just find my breath; I found a tiny green shoot pushing through broken ground. It was the first soft light of morning after a long, night.

The decision wasn't just to step back from the edge; it was to open my sails, catch the wind, and steer through these rough waters with a strong, steady guide inside me.

I had thought I had lost my mother. But Baba was always there — steady, silent, carrying both his grief and mine.

And now I saw:

Without me, how would my baby survive? For him, I am his only one.

Nikesh and Sweety were out there — living, laughing, mocking my pain.

But what was Addhu's fault? He didn't choose this.

I gave him life — and now, it's my sacred duty to give him a better one. A life filled with love, dignity, and strength. To raise him with values so he never becomes the man his father chose to be.

What about my sisters, who wept on my wedding day? What about Vishnu and Sujan — who always looked up to me?

In their eyes, I wasn't just a sister — I was strength, I was hope. What about Aama — who held my shattered pieces together with nothing but quiet kindness?

They all need me. They all love me.

They were the strong roots holding me up, the solid ground under my feet. And they deserved me whole—not a memory, not a story left unfinished. I will live—for them, and most of all—for the woman in the mirror, who refused to stay shattered.

God — do what You must. You've thrown storms at me, shattered me in places no one could see. But you forgot one thing: I'm still standing—not because I was never broken, but because I refused to stay shattered.

I want my voice back, not as a whisper, but as a loud river. I want my fire back, not as a dying spark, but as a bright, clearing flame.

I choose to live—fiercely, loudly, on my own damn terms.

A miracle didn't save me. A voice saved me. By a child who didn't just call me Mumma— He reminded me I'm still here. Pain didn't leave. But now, it walks beside my purpose—not in front of it.

This is not the end of my story. This is the fierce, glorious beginning of the life I chose.

And if you ever feel the ground crumbling beneath your feet, remember this: Your voice. Your purpose. Your inherent worth. They are your anchors. You are enough—to rise, to fight, to begin again.

I didn't rise like a warrior. I rose like a mother.

And that was enough.

To the one reading this—if you ever feel like falling, hold onto something that smells like life. Even if it's just a breath, a whisper, or your own name. You're not alone. I was there once.

And I rose.

High Heels Where Resilience Wears Hope

I did not rise with thunder loud,

Nor wrapped in the robes of a cheering crowd.

I rose in silence, breath by breath,

From pain, from loss, from near death.

I walked through fire in borrowed shoes,

Each blister is a testament to battles lost and won.

But the heels never broke—

Because neither did I.

I bent, I bled, I stumbled, I wept,

Yet never kneeled to what tried to end me.

They mistook my silence for surrender,

But I was only learning to roar softly.

I rose not crowned, but cracked and true,

With scars that shimmered morning dew.

Not as a phoenix, bold and grand—

But as a mother, a woman, who chose to stand.

Now I walk—not for applause,

Not for them—

But for the little voice that called me back,

For the girl in the mirror who finally said, "Enough."

For every woman still learning

She was never too much,

Never too little—

Just enough to rise.

These high heels aren't for show.

They are my armour.

Every step in them?

A rebellion. A revival. A return.

A Message from My Heart

If you've walked these pages with me, you've seen love and loss, laughter and tears, triumphs and trials. You've seen a little girl dream, a young woman struggle, and a mother fight to hold her world together. This is not just my story—it is a story of resilience, courage, and the unbreakable spirit that lives in each of us.

Life will test you. It will try to break you, silence you, and make you doubt your worth. But remember this: your story belongs to you. No one else can write it, no one else can define your path. You have the power to rise, even when the world expects you to fall. You can turn pain into strength, sorrow into wisdom, and fear into fuel.

To every woman who feels unseen, unheard, or undervalued—you are enough. To every soul who wonders if their dreams matter—you are worthy of chasing them. Your courage does not have to roar; even small, quiet acts of perseverance are victories that echo far beyond what you can see.

I write this not to close a chapter, but to open a door: for you, for me, for anyone who refuses to give up. Life will not always be gentle, but it will always be yours to live fully, boldly, and bravely. And if I could survive, rise, and reclaim my voice, so can you.

So stand tall. Speak your truth. Chase your dreams. Love fiercely. And when life shakes you, let it shake out the fear, not the fire inside.

Your story is waiting. and it's beautiful.

Muna Dadel

Acknowledgment

This book is born from a journey I never thought I would take—through love, loss, and the quiet strength that carried me forward. My Baba's unwavering love and silent tears were my anchor in the storms; my family's sacrifices shaped the person I became; and Aama, who stepped into our lives when I needed shelter the most, reminded me that hope can return in unexpected ways.

Most of all, I owe everything to my husband, V. Sairam—the one who held my hand when the world felt dark, who helped me find my voice again, and who believed in a life for me beyond survival. Together, we built a world filled with laughter, love, and light. Our daughter Saisha brought a new kind of joy into our lives, giving Adhyan a sister he adores, and our loyal GSD, Ghost, completed the picture of the family I once feared I had lost forever.

Looking back, the journey wasn't easy—but each step, each struggle, each tear brought me closer to this moment: a life truly lived, not just endured.

To my readers, thank you for walking alongside me. If you wish to know how I reached here, write to me—the story doesn't end with *High Heels*. The next chapter is waiting.